Learning about Language

Bringing a fresh and lively approach to language study, *Learning about Language* is an exciting collection of fun, creative activities and warm-up games that explore the multifaceted nature of the English language. For use in any primary classroom, this book will help develop the pupil's knowledge of how the English language works and will improve their ability to use language effectively.

Throughout the book, the author explains key features of the English language by arranging the volume alphabetically into sections, each of which explores a different linguistic feature. John Foster suggests enjoyable activities that will enable students to consolidate their learning and improve their communication skills through word play, and frequently uses rhyme to illustrate and elaborate on points made.

Areas covered include:

- Spelling, punctuation and grammar;
- Origin, meaning, similarities and differences of words, including homonyms, anagrams and synonyms;
- The explanation of particular uses of language for specific purposes;
- Humorous misuse of words, including malapropisms and spoonerisms;
- The inclusion of numerous opportunities for students to play with words by participating in word games and through their own writing.

With its unique and accessible approach to language study, *Learning about Language* provides teachers of English with a dynamic collection of resources that will be welcomed by educators and students alike.

John Foster taught English for twenty years before becoming a full time writer. He has written over 100 books for classroom use and is a highly regarded children's poet, anthologist and poetry performer.

Learning about Language

Activities for the primary classroom

John Foster

Routledge
Taylor & Francis Group

LONDON AND NEW YORK

First published 2012
by Routledge
2 Park Square, Milton Park, Abingdon, Oxon OX14 4RN

Simultaneously published in the USA and Canada
by Routledge
711 Third Avenue, New York, NY 10017

Routledge is an imprint of the Taylor & Francis Group, an informa business

British Library Cataloguing in Publication Data
A catalogue record for this book is available from the British Library

Library of Congress Cataloging in Publication Data
Foster, John, 1941 Oct. 12-
Learning about language : activities for the primary classroom / John Foster.
pages cm
Includes index.
ISBN 978-0-415-53680-6 (hbk.) -- ISBN 978-0-415-53681-3 (pbk.) --
ISBN 978-0-203-11116-1 (ebk.) 1. English language--Study and teaching
(Elementary)--Activity programs. I. Title.
LB1576.F645 2012
372.6'044--dc23
2012002381

ISBN: 978-0-415-53680-6 (hbk)
ISBN: 978-0-415-53681-3 (pbk)
ISBN: 978-0-203-11116-1 (ebk)

Typeset in Bembo
by Saxon Graphics Ltd, Derby

Printed and bound in Great Britain by
TJ International Ltd, Padstow, Cornwall

Contents

Introduction

Learning about language – activities for the primary classroom

Learning about Language – Activities for the primary classroom provides a comprehensive coverage of everything that the primary school pupil needs to know about the English language. The book provides teachers of literacy with clear explanations of the terms that pupils need to know, arranged alphabetically for ease of reference, together with details of activities that can be used to develop pupils' understanding of the English language.

A particular feature of the book is that it contains a number of poems, designed to present key information about features of language in a lively and original manner. The aim is to foster an interest in words and how they fit together, to provide ways of playing with words and to make exploring the English language fun.

Each section focuses on a different feature of the English language. The various sections

- examine subjects such as spelling, punctuation and grammar
- explore aspects of words such as their origin and meaning, their similarities and differences, e.g. homonyms, anagrams and synonyms
- explain particular uses of language, for example in the sections on clichés, idioms, metaphors and similes
- show how language is used humorously in jokes, puns and riddles and by poets using wordplay in forms such as limericks; also with sections on the humorous misuse of words – on malapropisms and spoonerisms
- include numerous opportunities for students to consolidate their learning in a variety of activities, including word games.

The book aims to provide teachers with detailed practical suggestions of activities that can be developed on the various language features. These ideas are grouped in a section entitled, for example, *Focus on nouns*, which shows how a lesson on nouns can be developed and provides ideas for activities designed to enable pupils to practise what they have learned and to demonstrate their understanding. The suggestions range from simple matching activities and arranging words in alphabetical order to coining words, making a dictionary of slang, writing acrostics and kennings, and solving riddles. Most of the sections include at least one activity sheet per topic, which can be photocopied or put on the whiteboard.

In addition to offering sufficient ideas for a whole lesson on a particular language topic, there is, where appropriate, a section entitled *Language opportunities*, containing suggestions as to how knowledge about language can be introduced in topic work or when a particular type of writing is being taught.

There are also suggestions for *Extension activities* for use with more able pupils.

The book, therefore, provides teachers of English, both specialists and non-specialists, with a lively bank of resources for learning about the English language.

Abbreviations

An abbreviation is a shortened form of either a word or a phrase.

Focus on abbreviations

Explain what an abbreviation is and how abbreviations are used.

- Abbreviations are used to shorten long words, e.g. HQ for headquarters, lab for laboratory, TV for television.
- They are used when writing a person's title, such as Mr, Ms, Dr or Rev., or a person's rank in the forces, such as Capt. or Col.
- They are widely used in textspeak, e.g. bbs for be back soon, plz for please. (See **Txtspk**, p. 173)

Language opportunities

When the class are learning about how to write invitations, explain that RSVP is an abbreviation of 'Répondez, s'il vous plaît', which means 'Reply, if you please.' It shows that a reply is expected.

In a lesson on letter-writing, point out that when they are writing a formal letter, they should use people's titles when addressing them. The titles are often abbreviations, such as Mr for Mister, Dr for Doctor and Rev. for Reverend.

You can also explain what a postscript is and that most people write the abbreviation PS when they add something at the bottom of a letter. This is short for the Latin term 'post scriptum', which means 'after writing'.

When discussing times of the day with the class, explain what a.m. and p.m. stand for and how they are abbreviations of the Latin expressions ante meridiem (before noon) and post meridiem (after noon).

Point out abbreviations that occur in information texts, such as e.g., i.e. and etc. Explain that e.g. means 'for example' and is short for the Latin term 'exempli gratia', that i.e. means 'that is' and is short for the Latin term 'id est', and that etc. is short for 'et cetera', a Latin term meaning 'and the rest'.

When looking at a detailed map, during a topic on the environment, point out the abbreviations that are used, for example PO for post office and PH for public house.

Extension activity

Activity sheet 1 – Abbreviations is an extension activity that can be used as appropriate with more able groups.

Activity sheet 1 – Abbreviations

Use a dictionary to help you to fill in the following table giving the meaning of the abbreviation and the Latin phrase for which it is short.

Abbreviation	Meaning	Latin phrase
AD		
a.m.		
e.g.		
etc.		
i.e.		
NB		
p.m.		
p.p.		
PS		
QED		
RIP		

Acrostics

An acrostic is a number of lines of writing in which certain letters of a word in each line together form a word.

Focus on acrostics

Explain what an acrostic is and then play the acrostics game in which you pick a subject, such as the weather. Make a list of words to do with the weather, such as rain, sunshine, gale, thunder, lightning, hurricane, etc. and then choose one of them, e.g hurricane. Write the word vertically down the side of the whiteboard and go round the class, asking the children in turn to supply a word or phrase beginning with the letters of the word 'hurricane', so that you build up an acrostic. Anyone who cannot think of a word or phrase simply says 'pass'. After the class have produced the acrostic of hurricane, they choose another word from the list of weather words.

Here's an acrostic one class wrote:

Houses blown away,
Umbrellas torn.
Raging storm
Ripping tiles off roofs.
Incredible damage,
Cars washed away,
Anxious mothers searching,
Nothing left standing.
Everywhere destruction.

Use **Activity sheet 2 – Acrostics.** Focus on James's acrostic. Ask what impression James gives of himself and discuss how this is achieved. Remind the class what adjectives are and explain that James has chosen a number of positive adjectives to describe himself. Encourage them to use dictionaries to find the meaning of words such as jocular (good humoured) and mercurial (lively), which are probably new to many of them.

Invite them to write an acrostic of their own either about their own name or the name of a friend or relative, choosing adjectives which give a positive impression of the person.

Focus on the acrostic 'Pirates'. Discuss how this differs from the acrostics which they have been looking at so far, because of the way each line begins 'P is for...', 'I is for...', and because the poet uses alliteration in each line. Ask the children which line they like the best. What is the overall impression of pirates that the poem gives?

Ask individuals to write their own acrostics about someone sinister such as a ghost, a zombie, an alien, an ogre or a goblin. Encourage them to use alliteration in their poems.

Extension activity

Ask individuals to look at the acrostic 'Winter'. What impression does the poem give of winter? Ask them to write down one or two adjectives which sum up the writer's view of winter. Discuss how this impression is given. Talk about how the poet uses personification – the giving of human characteristics to inanimate objects. For example, winter 'wraps cold arms' about the earth, the trees are described as 'numb', snow 'smothers' the fields. Focus on the powerful verbs that are used in each line – wraps, grips, shiver, smother, buried, glistening. Why are the icicles described as 'ropes'? What does this suggest?

Invite the pupils to write their own acrostics about another season or about a month. Before they begin, ask them to decide what impression they want to give of that particular season or month and to write down one or two adjectives that sum up that impression. Encourage them to focus on using powerful verbs and to use personification in their poems.

Jolly, jovial and jocular
Attractive, amiable and ambitious
Mercurial, mesmerising and magnificent
Energetic, elegant and eloquent
Strong, sensitive and spectacular.

James's acrostic consists of a number of adjectives, which give a favourable impression of him. Write a similar acrostic about your name.

Pirates

P is for pistols and plunder, for parrots and prisoners walking the plank.
I is for isolated islands where they've buried their gold.
R is for ruthless and rascal, for ruffian and rum.
A is for Avast! Ahoy! and Abandon ship!
T is for terrorise, tattoo and treasure.
E is for emeralds, ear-rings and eye-patch.
S is for sinister, savage and skull.

The acrostic about pirates uses a lot of alliteration. Write an acrostic in which you describe someone sinister such as an alien, a ghost, a vampire, a goblin, an ogre or a zombie. Choose your words carefully and try to include some alliteration.

Winter

Winter wraps the earth in its cold arms.
Icy frost grips the ground.
Numb trees shiver in the bitter wind.
Thick sheets of snow smother the fields.
Everything is buried beneath a white cloak.
Ropes of icicles hang from gutters, glistening.

Write an acrostic either about another season or about one of the months. Before you begin, decide what impression you want your poem to give of the particular season or month.

Alliteration

Alliteration is the use of several words together that all begin with the same letter or sound.

For example: 'The whistling wind whipped up the waves.'

Language opportunities

There are opportunities to focus on alliteration when you are studying tongue-twisters (see p. 178) and when studying the acrostic 'Pirates' (see p. 8).

Another opportunity to focus on alliteration is when you are studying persuasive writing. Many advertisers use alliteration in order to make their slogans more memorable. For example, the Country Life butter advertisement: You'll never put a better bit of butter on your knife.

You can also point to the use of alliteration in the names of characters in the books they are reading, such as Helga Hufflepuff in the Harry Potter books and Winnie the Witch, and in the names of characters in comics and comic strips, such as Freddie Flintstone, Desperate Dan, Mickey Mouse, Daffy Duck and Bugs Bunny.

You can also focus on alliteration when you are looking at classic poetry, which often contains examples of alliteration, such as Tennyson's 'The Eagle'.

> He clasps the crag with crooked hands;
> Close to the sun in lonely lands,
> Ring'd with the azure world, he stands.
>
> The wrinkled sea beneath him crawls;
> He watches from his mountain walls,
> And like a thunderbolt he falls.

Alphabet

An alphabet is a writing system in which symbols are used to represent the individual sounds made by the words in a language.

Focus on the alphabet

Talk about different writing systems. Explain that the earliest writing systems were based on pictures. English uses a system based on letters which are used to represent the sounds made by words.

Remind them that the English alphabet has twenty-six letters. Twenty-one are consonants *b c d f g h j k l m n p q r s t v w x y z* and the other five are vowels *a e i o u*. Explain that all English words have a vowel in them (or the letter *y* acting as a vowel).

A problem with English is that there are more sounds than letters. So letters have to be combined in order to spell certain sounds. This is particularly the case with vowel sounds because there are twenty vowel sounds and only five vowel letters.

Explain how alphabetical order is used in indexes and dictionaries. Write the following words on the board: know cows little prefer all mice I eat however seeds brown grass. Explain that put in alphabetical order the words will make a sentence. Can they unscramble the sentence? The answer is: 'All brown cows eat grass; however, I know little mice prefer seeds.'

Invite groups to play the **Alphabet Game**. The aim is to answer questions using words that begin with a certain letter of the alphabet. The first player chooses a letter, for example *S*. The other players begin by asking a question such as, 'What are you going to do?' The first player has to reply by saying three things beginning with *s*. For example, 'I'm going to eat sausages, play snooker and sing songs.' Another player then asks, 'Where are you going to do them?' The first player has to answer using three words beginning with the letter *s*. For example, 'I'm going to eat sausages on the sofa, play snooker on the sideboard and sing songs in Southend.' Another player then asks, 'Who are you going to do them with?' Again, the first player has to answer using three words beginning with *s*. For example, 'I'm going eat sausages on the sofa with Sonia, play snooker on the sideboard with Stan and sing songs in Southend with Samir.' If the other players can think of another follow-up question, they ask it. For example, 'When are you going to do these things?' Again, the first person has to answer with three words beginning with *s*. For example, 'On Sunday I'm going to eat sausages on the sofa with Sonia, etc.' Questions continue until no one can think of anything further to ask or the first player cannot think of answers. Then it is someone else's turn.

Explain the rules of **Taboo** and then ask groups to play. One of the players chooses a letter and acts as questioner. In turn the questioner asks each of the other players a different question. The question can be about anything at all. In their answer they have to avoid using the chosen letter. The answers have to make sense and must be given immediately. At the start, each player has a set number of points, e.g. 12. Every time a player makes a mistake, she loses a point. The winner is the person who has the most points left at the end of the game.

Invite more able pupils to write lipograms (see *Extension activity*).

You can end the focus on the alphabet by telling the class about some interesting words.

There are a number of words which have their letters in alphabetical order, including *abhors, almost* and *begins*.

The word *spoonfeed* has its letters in reverse alphabetical order.

Fickleheaded and *fiddledeedee* are the longest words containing only letters from the first half of the alphabet.

Uncopyrightable is the only fifteen-letter word which has fifteen different letters in it.

Language opportunities

When teaching about the Egyptians and how they used hieroglyphics, you can compare their writing system with other writing systems.

Extension activity – lipograms

Explain what a lipogram is: a piece of writing which omits a letter of the alphabet. Read them the poem 'I promise', which is a lipogram in which the poet has avoided the use of any words containing the letter *a*. Then invite them to try to write a lipogram of their own, either a story or a poem.

I promise
I promise I'll be good.
I'll do the things I should.
I'll pick my clothes up off the floor.
I'll do every other chore.
I will do my homework too.
I will listen closely to you.
Why do you look with such surprise?
I need the pocket money rise.

Anagrams

An anagram is a word or phrase consisting of letters which can be rearranged to form another word.

Focus on anagrams

Explain what an anagram is and write the word *pins* on the board. Show how the letters of *pins* can be rearranged to make the words *spin*, *nips* and *snip*. Write *snap* on the board and ask them which words are anagrams of it (*pans*, *naps*, *span*).

Put the two verses of the poem 'A ragman's puzzle' on the board. Focus on the first verse and discuss the anagrams in each line.

Write the words *mane*, *ramp*, *pier* and *limes* on the board. Ask them to write down any anagrams of each one. The answers are: *name/mean/amen*, *pram*, *ripe* and *smile/miles/slime*.

Then focus on the second verse. Ask whether they can spot the difference between the two verses? Draw out the answer that, in the second verse, the word which is the anagram also spells the first word if read backwards!

Put this list of words on the board: *buns nuts deer pots trap tons tips taps keel guns*. Explain that each forms a new word when written backwards. Ask them to write the words backwards to see what words they form.

A ragman's puzzle
Why is a mate like a team?
Why is a spot like stop?
Why are capes like a space?
Why are hops like a shop?
Why are pets like a step?
Why is a loop like a pool?
Why is peels like sleep?
Why is loot like a tool?

Extension activity

Give each member of the group a copy of **Activity sheet 3** and ask them to work out the anagrams in each line of the poem 'Anagram antics'.

The answers are: *races* scare, *stone* notes, *tears* stare, *votes* stove, *loop* pool, *bread* beard, *late* tale, *leap* peal, *reap* pear, *hose* shoe.

Finish by asking them to see if they can find the answers to 'Work it out'. The answers are: *listen, the Morse Code, vocabulary, decimal point, Monday, twelve plus one, slot machines, conversation.*

Activity sheet 3 – Anagram antics

The word in italics in each line of the poem 'Anagram antics' is an anagram of another word. There is a clue in the rest of the line to help you to work out what that word is. For example, the answer to 'Mix up *races* to give someone a fright' is *scare*. Write down your answers.

Anagram antics

Mix up *races* to give someone a fright.
Make *stone* into messages you write.

Wipe away *tears* then give me a look.
Turn *gape* into what you will find in a book.

Untie *loop* to find a place to dive in.
Knead *bread* into hairs that grow on a chin.

Stir up *late* into a story to tell.
Shuffle *leap* into the sound of a bell.

Spin *reap* into a fruit to eat.
Juggle *hose* into what to put on your feet.

Work it out

Use the clues in each pair of lines to work out what words are anagrams of the words and phrases in italics.

Silent is an anagram of what you must do
When someone starts to talk to you.

Here come dots sends messages, it's true.
It's a way of sending a signal to you.

Rearrange *a vocal ruby* to show
All the words you already know.

I'm a dot in place is what you use when
You're putting a fraction in a base of ten.

When it's an anagram of *dynamo* you seek,
Just think of one of the days of the week.

I too make thirteen! What you must do
Is to rearrange *eleven plus two.*

Lost cash in me? You'll find me displayed
To tempt you in an amusement arcade.

Voices rant on appears to be
What we have when you talk to me.

Borrowings

Borrowings are words from other languages that have become part of the English language.

Focus on borrowings

Prepare for the lesson by making cards with words on them together with their origins (make an even number of cards with enough for each member of the class to have one): *egg* Old Norse; *sky* Old Norse; *restaurant* French; *river* French; *cruise* Dutch; *skate* Dutch; *tea* Chinese; *ketchup* Chinese; *rucksack* German; *spanner* German; *sugar* Arabic; *lemon* Arabic; *boomerang* Aboriginal; *dingo* Aboriginal; *myth* Greek; *orchestra* Greek; *bungalow* Hindi; *dinghy* Hindi; *piano* Italian; *solo* Italian; *karate* Japanese; *sudoku* Japanese; *circus* Latin; *maximum* Latin; *mosquito* Spanish; *canyon* Spanish; *gymkhana* Urdu; *khaki* Urdu; *caravan* Persian; *tiara* Persian; *bairn* Scottish; *glen* Scottish.

You will also need a map of the world and some drawing pins.

Explain that the oldest words in English are Old English. This was the language spoken by the Anglo-Saxons. Old English words include simple ones such as *the, to, a, be, from* and *with* and common words such as *thing, man, do, say, get* and *have*. As time passed, words were borrowed from other languages. The Vikings brought Old Norse words, such as *egg, law, leg* and *sky*. The Normans brought French words and many Latin words. Nowadays the English language consists of words from many different sources – from European languages, such as French, Spanish, Italian and German, to other languages from around the world, such as Hindi, Urdu, Arabic and Chinese.

Put up the map of the world. Give every child a card, then get each in turn to read out the word on the card and its origin and then to come up and pin the card onto the map to show where the different countries are that have given words to English.

Play the **Memory Game**. This is a game for two players using the cards you prepared. It begins with all the cards spread out face down on the table.

The first player turns over two cards. If the two cards show words that originated from the same language, she picks up the pair and has another go. If they do not match, she turns them back over and the second player has a turn. The game continues till there are no cards left. The winner is the person with the most cards.

Play **Borrowings Snap**. This is another game for two players using the cards you prepared. The cards are shuffled and each player is dealt an equal number of them. They take it in turns to put down a card, and when two cards containing words that originated from the same language are put down they have to shout Snap. The person who shouts Snap first picks up all the cards. The winner is the person with the most cards at the end of the game.

Ask the children to complete **Activity sheet 4 – Borrowings**.

The words in this list have all come into English from other languages: *anorak bandit cargo delicious envelope famine garage halt idiot judo kiosk lunar melody narrate obstinate pyjamas quit robot sleigh typhoon uniform vanilla wigwam xylophone yodel zombie.*

Use a dictionary to help complete the chart, saying what type of word each one is, what it means and what language it comes from.

Word	Type	Meaning	Origin
anorak	noun	a warm waterproof jacket	Inuit

Clichés

A cliché is a word or phrase that has been used so often that it has lost most of its force and effectiveness, e.g. I'm thrilled to bits, I'm over the moon.

Focus on clichés

■ Read the poem 'Are you as quiet as a mouse?' Explain what a cliché is and discuss the clichés that are used in the poem.

Are you as quiet as a mouse?
Do you sleep like a log?
Are you as cunning as a fox?
Are you treated like a dog?

Can you swim like a fish?
Do you sometimes smell a rat?
Are you as greedy as a pig?
Are you as blind as a bat?

Explain that if we use clichés too much, our writing becomes dull. Make copies of **Activity sheet 5 – Clichés** for the pupils to complete.

Make a list of clichés that are used to express feelings: happiness, e.g. I was over the moon; disappointment, e.g. I was as sick as a parrot; fear, e.g. I was shaking like a leaf; nervousness, e.g. I was a bag of nerves; sadness, e.g. I was down in the dumps; delight, e.g. as pleased as punch; anxiety, e.g. like a cat on a hot tin roof.

Write the list of clichés on a large sheet of paper to put on the classroom wall. Put up this notice beside the list to remind them to avoid using clichés when they write:

Advice to Young Writers
Clichés should be avoided like the plague.

Discuss how sports commentators, football managers and players frequently use clichés. Together with the class, make a list of football clichés and put it on the board.

Examples of football clichés include: It's a funny old game; it's game of two halves; to be under the cosh; at the end of the day; hit the woodwork; completely gutted; over the moon; we were/they were robbed; be in with a shout; we/they gave one hundred per cent; worked their socks off; he won't score a better goal than that; it wasn't to be; take it one game at a time; not get carried away.

Then invite pairs to prepare to act out a post-match interview in which a manager or a player talks about a game that has just ended. The aim is for them to include as many of the clichés as possible in their interview. Invite some of the pairs to act out their interviews to the class.

Extension activity

Invite more able groups to undertake the Cliché challenge. The other children in the class could be given copies of the winning sentence (see below) and asked to highlight the clichés in it.

Cliché challenge

This is a word game for any number of players. The aim of the game is to write a sentence containing as many clichés as possible within a set time limit, e.g. fifteen minutes. At the end of the game, count how many clichés your sentence contains. The person with the most clichés in a sentence is the winner.

Here's an example of a winning sentence from a previous game:

'I was boiling hot and I was sweating like a pig, but it was a race against time, so I seized the opportunity with both hands, since it was now or never, and with my heart in my mouth, hoping against hope that I'd live to see another day, I took the plunge and waited with bated breath to see if I'd hit the target.'

Activity sheet 5 – Clichés

Each of these comparisons is a cliché. Think of an alternative, which is not a cliché, and write it next to the cliché. The first one has been done for you.

1. As fast as greased lightning	As fast as a speeding comet
2. As slow as a snail	
3. As strong as an ox	
4. As light as a feather	
5. As hot as the sun	
6. As tough as old boots	
7. As slippery as an eel	
8. As soft as silk	
9. As hard as nails	
10. As weak as a kitten	
11. As red as a beetroot	
12. As white as a sheet	

Coined words

A coined word or phrase is one that the writer made up.

Focus on coining

Make copies of **Activity sheet 6 – Coined words**. Explain what is meant by a coined word and that Lewis Carroll's poem 'Jabberwocky' contains many of them, then read the poem to the pupils.

Point out that although it is full of nonsense words, it is still possible to make some sense of the poem from the way the words fit together to form sentences and the way that Lewis Carroll has created words which echo sounds and, therefore, suggest meanings. Explain that Lewis Carroll himself supplied interpretations of some of the words. For example, he suggested that *slithy* meant lithe and slimy and that *mimsy* meant flimsy and miserable.

Remind them what a glossary is – a list of words and phrases connected to a particular subject together with an explanation of their meanings, arranged in alphabetical order. Ask the pupils to produce a glossary of the words Lewis Carroll made up, together with their interpretations of their meanings.

Extension activity

Ask pupils in groups or pairs to suggest meanings for this A to Z of coined words. Then invite them to coin some words of their own and produce a class dictionary of coined words and their meanings. Remind them to say what part of speech the word is.

arrowgent (n.) blinkmanship (n.) conpose (vb.) driggon (n.) elepant (vb.) flitterly (adv.) glumlin (n.) higgle (vb.) itter (vb.) jocal (adj.) klumpish (adj.) murgle (vb.) namesnake (n.) orpishly (adv.) plotate (vb.) quandrous (adj.) rumbluster (vb.) stewhif (n.) tintacular (adj.) uggle (vb.) vulturifly (vb.) X-rain (n.) yawdle (vb.) zaffish (adj.)

Jabberwocky

Lewis Carroll

’Twas brillig, and the slithy toves
Did gyre and gimble in the wabe;
All mimsy were the borogroves
And the mome raths outgrabe.

Beware the Jabberwock, my son!
The jaws that bite, the claws that catch!
Beware the Jubjub bird and shun
The frumious Bandersnatch!

He took his vorpal sword in hand:
Long time the manxome foe he sought –
So rested he by the Tumtum tree,
And stood awhile in thought.

And as in uffish thought he stood,
The Jabberwock with eyes of flame,
Came whiffling through the tulgey wood,
And burbled as it came!

One two! One two! and through and through
The vorpal blade went snicker-snack!
He left it dead, and with its head
He went galumphing back.

“And hast thou slain the Jabberwock!
Come to my arms, my beamish boy!
O frabjous day! Callooh! Callay!”
He chortled in his joy.

’Twas brillig, and the slithy toves
Did gyre and gimble in the wabe;
All mimsy were the borogroves
And the mome raths outgrabe.

Dialect

A dialect is a type of English that is spoken by a particular group of people.

Focus on dialect

Explain what a dialect is and how a dialect has its own words and expressions and its own grammar rules. Most dialects are spoken by people in particular areas of the country, so there is, for example, a Geordie dialect spoken in the north-east of England, a Liverpool dialect and a Cornish dialect.

Explain that when we write in school we use Standard English and that there are a number of grammar rules, which we must follow, that may be different from the grammar of any dialect we speak.

Put a copy of **Standard English – some grammar rules** on the board and discuss the differences between the two accounts. Then go through the various rules. Either give each pupil a copy for reference or keep one on the classroom wall. You can then focus on a particular rule as the opportunity arises. (See *Language opportunities* below.)

Standard English – some grammar rules

Here are two versions of someone describing an incident in a football match. One is in dialect. One is in Standard English.

'We was watching the match and one of them big guys from their team gets sent off. He start swearing and saying it ain't fair and that he never done nothing wrong.'

'We were watching the match and one of those big guys from their team got sent off.
He started swearing and saying it isn't fair and that he didn't do anything wrong.'

Talk about the differences between the two versions and discuss the grammar rules (below).

Standard English rules

1. In Standard English you cannot say 'we was' or 'you was'. It must always be 'we were' or 'you were'.

2. In Standard English you cannot say 'them big guys'. It must be 'those big guys'.

3. In Standard English, when speaking or writing about the past, you must use verbs with their proper past tense form or past tense ending. You cannot say or write 'he gets sent off', it must be 'he got sent off'. Similarly, it must be 'he started swearing', not 'he start swearing'.

4. In Standard English, you cannot use 'ain't'. It must always be 'isn't'.

5. In Standard English, you should not use an expression that has a double negative in it. It is wrong to say 'He never done nothing'. It should be 'He didn't do anything'.

Language opportunities

You can use the opportunities that occur when pupils use dialect forms in their written work to focus on one or more of the rules, as appropriate.

Dictionary

A dictionary is a book of words in their alphabetical order, giving the meaning of each word, its part of speech, pronunciation and derivation.

Focus on dictionaries

Explain that the words in a dictionary are arranged in alphabetical order.

Use **Activity sheet 7 – Dictionary order** to explain exactly how words are ordered in a dictionary, and to help them understand what the order is, by putting lists of words in order as they would appear in a dictionary. Make sure they understand the importance of looking at the second and third letters of a word, as well as the first.

Put a copy of the poem on the board. Ask them to think about dictionary order, to decide which of the words would come first and to write Yes or No in answer to each question. The answers are: 1 Yes, 2 No, 3 Yes, 4 No, 5 Yes, 6 Yes, 7 No, 8 No.

1. Does bake come before book?
2. Does crab come before cook?
3. Does water come before wet?
4. Does jingle come before jet?
5. Does bread come before butter?
6. Does murmur come before mutter?
7. Does plumber come before plane?
8. Does trouble come before train?

Use **Activity sheet 8 – How to use a dictionary** to teach the pupils about the information which a dictionary gives about a word. Encourage them to practise using a dictionary by playing the games **Find the Word, Dictionary Quiz, Beat the Teacher** and **Fact or Fiction**.

Find the Word

In this game, you give the children a word and they have to race to find what page it is on in a dictionary. The winner then reads out what part of speech the word is, its meaning and what its origin. You can link this in with topic work by choosing words that they will encounter while studying that topic.

Dictionary Quiz

This is a game for two players. Each person has a dictionary. They take it in turns to choose a word. The first player tells the other person three things about the word – what part of speech it is, what letter of the alphabet the word begins with or ends with, and what its meaning is. If the person doesn't guess the word from this information then they are given further clues.

For example, the first player might pick the word 'bright' and say 'I'm thinking of an adjective. It begins with *b*. It means "shining strongly"'. If the other person doesn't guess the word from this information, the questioner might give other clues, such as, 'The same word also means clever', 'It has six letters' or 'It rhymes with fight.'

Beat the Teacher

Groups take it in turns to pick a word from the dictionary, to say what the word means and to ask the teacher what the word is. Every time the teacher gets the word wrong the group scores a point. The teacher can ask for further information about the word: How many letters has it? What part of speech is it? What is its origin? What does it rhyme with? Every time the teacher asks a question another point is scored. The turn continues until the teacher gets the right word or has to give up. If the teacher has to give up, the group scores an extra five points. The group with the most points at the end of the game is the winner. Note: Although you may know the word that a group has chosen, you may decide to act dumb in order to make them look more closely at what information the dictionary gives about a particular word.

Fact or Fiction

This is a game for more able pupils to play in groups of three. One group chooses a word from a dictionary which they think the other group won't know. Then they think of two other meanings for the word that sound plausible. They tell another group the three meanings and the second group has to say which one is fact and which two are fiction.

For example, let's say a group choose the word *repel* which means *drive back*. They then have to think of two other definitions which sound plausible, such *repair* or *repeat*.

Extension activity

Read about the origin of the word 'clue' and invite more able children to look up the origins of the words in the list. See **Activity sheet 8 – Using a dictionary.**

Language opportunities

When studying a topic, encourage pupils to develop their dictionary skills by looking up new words they come across and to write the word and its meaning on a piece of paper and display it on the topic wordlist that you have pinned up on the noticeboard. Alternatively, they can type the word and its meaning onto the computer and add it to a topic wordlist that you print out and give to them at the conclusion of the topic.

Activity sheet 7 – Dictionary order

The words in a dictionary are arranged in alphabetical order. To work out where to find a word in a dictionary, you often have to look at the first two or three letters of a word.

First letters

Put these words in the order in which you would find them in a dictionary.

1. leg bone shoulder knee arm ....

2. ghost vampire tomb coffin blood ....

3. guitar drum keyboard saxophone piano ....

4. pea carrot turnip potato lettuce ....

5. story myth legend tale fable ....

First and second letters

When words begin with the same letter, you have to look at the first and second letters to work out their dictionary order. Put these lists of words into their dictionary order.

1. lock luck label letter little ....

2. foe fiend frame flee famous ....

3. bottle broom bang berry butter ....

4. trip towel thing table tickle ....

5. sword smile stick slope snake ....

First, second and third letters

When the first and second letters of words are the same, you have to look at the third letters as well to work out their dictionary order. Put these lists of words into their dictionary order.

1. grip grasp grunt ground gravel ....

2. break bridge brave breeze brook ....

3. sting study strap stagger steady ....

4. cling clatter clutch clever clock ....

5. injection index inch invisible information ....

A dictionary tells you several things about a word:

- how the word is spelt
- what type of word it is, for example a noun or a verb
- the different forms of the word, for example 'help', 'helped' and 'helping'
- what the word means and, if it has more than one meaning, what the different meanings are
- how the word is used, for example if it is slang.

Here is the entry for the word 'clot' from the *Collins School Dictionary*:

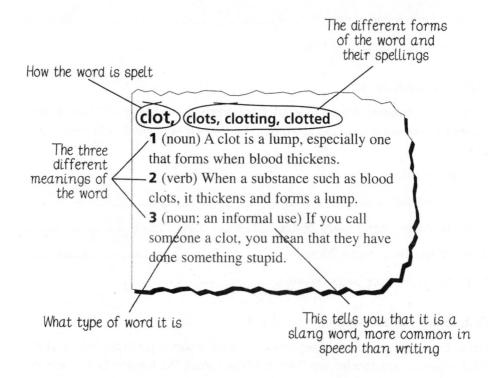

The different forms
of the word and
their spellings

How the word is spelt

clot, **clots, clotting, clotted**

The three
different
meanings of
the word

1 (noun) A clot is a lump, especially one that forms when blood thickens.

2 (verb) When a substance such as blood clots, it thickens and forms a lump.

3 (noun; an informal use) If you call someone a clot, you mean that they have done something stupid.

What type of word it is

This tells you that it is a
slang word, more common in
speech than writing

Activity sheet 8 – Using a dictionary (continued)

Word origins

Some dictionaries also explain the origins of words. Here is the entry for the word 'clue' from such a dictionary:

> The word **clue** is a modern spelling of the old word **clew**, 'a ball of thread'. The idea here is of string or thread being used to guide a person out of a maze by tracing a path through it. The most famous example is that of the Greek hero Theseus, who killed the monstrous bull-headed Minotaur in its lair and then escaped from the Labyrinth, an underground maze of tunnels. He was able to do this because the princess Ariadne gave him a ball of string which he unravelled as he went in and followed back to find his way out again.

Find out the origin of these words: *siren salary steeplechase sideburns slogan Thursday marathon grenade bonfire.*

Epitaphs

An epitaph is a piece of writing inscribed on a gravestone. Some epitaphs take the form of a verse.

Focus on epitaphs

Explain what an epitaph is and how it can take the form of a short poem. Put some examples on the whiteboard and show how an epitaph can be two, four or five lines long, e.g. John Brown (2 lines), Mr Lee (4 lines), Sandra Slater (5 lines).

Talk about each one in turn. What makes the epitaph funny? Point out how John Brown's epitaph is based round a pun on the word 'cavity'. What makes the other epitaphs funny?

John Brown – A dentist
Stranger approach this spot with gravity:
John Brown is filling his last cavity.

Jonathan Pease
Under the sod and under the trees
Lies the body of Jonathan Pease.
He is not here. There's only the pod.
Pease shelled out and went to God.

John Penny
Remember if cash thou art
In want of any
Dig 4 feet deep
And thou will find a Penny.

Mr Lee

Here lies a teacher Mr Lee
Who said, 'You'll be the death of me!'
And sitting at his desk one day
He gave a sigh and passed away.

Sandra Slater

Here lies what's left of Sandra Slater,
Who poked her pet – an alligator –
Forgetting that to tease or bait her
Might annoy an alligator.
Alas, the alligator ate her.

Use **Activity sheet 9 – Epitaphs** and ask the children to complete the epitaphs in pairs and then to write epitaphs of their own. If they get stuck because they cannot think of a rhyme, encourage them to use a rhyming dictionary.

Language opportunities

When you are doing a topic on the local environment, talk about churches and churchyards. Point out that gravestones have inscriptions on them and that they may be epitaphs and that these may be either quotations or original verses. Use the opportunity this provides for them to do research on the computer to find some unusual epitaphs such as Spike Milligan's 'I told you I was ill'.

Work with a partner and complete the following epitaphs:

1. In memory of William White
   Who did not stop at a red light...

2. Here lies the body of Marmaduke Hyde...

3. Here lies a careless girl called Kate...

4. In memory of a boy called Joe...

5. Beneath this stone Miss Ketchup lies...

Write an epitaph of your own your own. You could write about:

1. a person such as a teacher, a cook, an inventor, a weather forecaster or a zookeeper

2. a person with an unusual surname, such as Tommy Hawk, Betty Beetroot or Percy Pies

3. a nursery rhyme character, such as Old King Cole or a character from a traditional tale, such as Cinderella

4. an imaginary creature, such as an ogre called Ollie the Ogre or a dragon called Firesnorter.

Formal language

Formal language is used in schools and colleges and in business and government, for both speech and writing. The formal language used by teachers, politicians, television newsreaders and business people is known as Standard English.

Focus on formal and informal speech

Discuss how the way you speak varies according to the situation and to whom you are speaking.

When you are in the playground or out with your friends in an informal situation you will speak in a chatty, conversational way.

Read to the pupils how Dean told a friend about how Nasser broke a classroom window:

> 'We were playing footie and Naz gave the ball a right whack. It smacked against the tree and crashed straight through the window of Jacko's classroom. We all scarpered 'cause we knew Jacko would do his nut.'

Then read them how Dean told his teacher about the incident:

> 'We were playing football and Nasser kicked the ball so hard that it bounced off the tree and went through the window of Mr Jackson's classroom. We ran off because we knew Mr Jackson would be very angry.'

Talk about the differences and how Dean uses playground slang terms such as 'footie' for 'football', 'a right whack' for 'a hard kick', 'scarpered' for 'ran away' and 'do his nut' for 'be very angry'. Discuss how these slang terms are changed when he speaks Standard English to his teacher.

Invite them in pairs to role play the following situations:

A girl talks to a friend about what she did at the weekend.
She tells a teacher about what she did at the weekend.

A boy tells to a police officer about an accident he witnessed.
He tells a friend about the same accident.

A girl tells a parent how she plans to spend £100 left to her by a great-aunt.
She tells a friend what she plans to do with the money.

Make copies of **Activity sheet 10 – Informal speech** for individuals or pairs to complete. It presents a number of colloquial expressions and asks the pupils to write what they mean.

Language opportunities

Reading a play or getting the children to write playscripts offers a good opportunity for focusing on formal and informal speech.

Teaching letter-writing provides an opportunity to focus on formal and informal language. Point out that the informal conversational language used in letters and e-mails to friends is very different from the formal language you would use when writing, for example, to make an enquiry or a complaint.

Similarly, when the children are drafting invitations and replies to invitations, discuss how the invitations and replies are written in formal language.

Activity sheet 10 – Informal speech

Here are some expressions which are used in everyday informal conversations. Write down what they mean. The first one has been done for you.

1. A close shave	a narrow escape
2. At a loose end	
3. Get your skates on	
4. Give the thumbs up	
5. Go ballistic	
6. Go down like a lead balloon	
7. Have forty winks	
8. Lead up the garden path	
9. Let the cat out of the bag	
10. Lose your rag	
11. In the nick of time	
12. No worries	
13. Not half	
14. Pull your socks up	
15. Turn a blind eye	

Grammar

How the words in a language work together in speech and in writing is called the structure of the language. This structure and the rules governing it are called its grammar.

Focus on word order

Explain what the grammar of a language is and that it tells us how the words of a language are joined together to make sentences. In English this is done by word order and changing the form of words, e.g. by changing the tense of a verb from 'see' to 'saw'.

Put the verse 'Yesterday saw Robin I' on the board and talk about how important word order is to meaning. Point out how the words in the sentences in this verse are in the wrong order, so it doesn't make sense. If you rearrange them, it does!

> Yesterday saw Robin I.
> Robin to said 'Hi!' I.
> Replied me Robin to,
> 'Too nice see to you.'

Focus on sentences

Explain that there are four types of sentence.

> Statement: We're going to be late.
> Question: Where are my shoes?
> Command: Shut the front door after you.
> Exclamation: How silly!

Statements, questions and commands are far more common than exclamations.

Play the game **Take a Chance,** which is about different types of sentences.

You have to prepare for the game by making twenty-four small cards. Eight are statement cards with the following statements written on them:

Make a statement about the weather.
Make a statement about school.
Make a statement about food.
Make a statement about a TV programme.
Make a statement about a film.
Make a statement about a book.
Make a statement about a full stop.
Make a statement about a comma.

Eight are question cards with the following questions written on them:

What did you do yesterday?
Why do we recycle things?
Where do you live?
When does it get dark?
What is your favourite colour?
Who are you sitting next to?
How old are you?
Have you any brothers or sisters?

Eight are command cards with the following commands written on them:

Recite a poem or rhyme.
Tell a joke.
Give an example of an abbreviation.
Say a sentence with a simile in it.
Name a play by William Shakespeare.
Perform a charade about a book title.
Explain how to boil an egg.
Give an example of alliteration.

How to play: Shuffle each set of cards and lay them out in three piles. One person throws a dice. If you get 1 or 2, take a statement card. If you get 3 or 4, take a question card. If you get a 5 or 6, take a command card. Do what the card tells you, then put it back at the bottom of the pile.

Discuss how sentences can be divided into simple sentences and complex sentences. Statements, questions and exclamations have a *subject*, which usually tells you what the sentence is about.

Write this sentence on the board: 'The boy caught a fish.' Point out that the subject of the sentence is the boy. Explain that sentences normally contain a verb. Simple sentences have only one verb, in this case *caught*.

Explain that complex sentences have several verbs. Write this sentence on the board: 'When he was fishing in the lake, the boy caught a fish, which was the biggest he had ever caught, so he photographed it, before he threw it back.'

Discuss how the sentence has five separate sections in it, each section having its own verb. These sections are known as clauses.

There is a main clause, which in this case is 'the boy caught the fish'. All the other clauses are subordinate clauses. They are joined to the main clause either by conjunctions or by the relative pronouns *which* or *who*.

Parts of speech

Explain that words can be divided into word classes according to the way they are used in sentences. There are eight main word classes in English: nouns, verbs, adjectives, adverbs, pronouns, prepositions, conjunctions and articles. These are also known as the parts of speech.

Nouns

A noun is a word which is the name of a person, place or thing.

What is a noun?
A noun is the name of anything,
like *car* or *cat* or *coat* or *ring*.
A noun is the name of a person too,
like *Jason, Wasim, Jill* or *Sue*.
A noun is also the name of a place –
Pakistan, Glasgow, Mars or *Space*.
A noun's any kind of naming word –
bluebottle, Bill, Bolton, bird.

Put a copy of the poem 'What is a noun?' on the whiteboard and ask the pupils what are the differences between the nouns listed in the second, fourth and sixth lines. Draw out the point that the nouns listed in the second line are known as **common nouns** because each one is a general label given to an object, animal or thing.

As a class, make a list of common nouns which we use to label different forms of transport, e.g. ship boat yacht plane helicopter bus car bicycle lorry van taxi.

Then ask individuals or groups to make a list of common nouns we use to label different fruit or vegetables or different clothes.

The nouns in the second line are the names of people, and the nouns in the third line are the names of places. Explain that the names we use for particular people, places or animals are called **proper nouns** and that a proper noun always begins with a capital letter. Ask: Which are the two proper nouns in the last line of the poem?

Ask individuals or groups to invent some new proper nouns by imagining they are manufacturers who are about to launch new products. Invite them to suggest a catchy new name for a product such as a computer game in which knights battle against monsters, a new kite, a skateboard with a new shape, a remote controlled helicopter, a new scooter, a toy robot.

A noun alphabet book

Ask pairs to work together to produce a noun alphabet book about school, like the ones young children have, consisting of a common noun for each letter of the alphabet. For example, on the page for A you might put *a*rithmetic, *a*rt or *a*ssembly. For B you might put *b*reak, *b*ook or *b*rainstorm and so on.

Learning opportunities

During a lesson in which you are discussing families or family trees, remind the pupils that the names of people are proper nouns and that they should always start with a capital letter.

Similarly, in a lesson on the local environment, in which you are drawing attention to place names, remind the pupils that the names of places are proper nouns and they always start with a capital letter.

Collective nouns

A collective noun is a word that describes a particular group of animals, people or things.

Focus on collective nouns

Explain what a collective noun is and ask the children if they can give examples of collective nouns for a group of animals (e.g. a herd of cows), of people (e.g. a crowd of people) or of things (e.g. a bunch of keys).

Give out **Activity sheet 11 – Collective nouns** and ask the children to complete it.

Activity sheet 11 – Collective nouns

Match the animals to the collective noun that describes a group of them
by drawing a line to join the animals with the correct collective noun.
The first one has been done for you.

flock	lions
swarm	fish
litter	sheep
team	puppies
pack	snakes
gaggle	gorillas
cast	ants
herd	bees
school	geese
army	horses
pride	wolves
band	cows

Extension activity

Here are some other collective nouns. What groups do they refer to? Write sentences which include each of them. Use a dictionary to help you, if necessary.

For example: 'The ring of spectators clapped loudly.'

audience congregation horde bunch clump cluster squadron fleet set ring

Activity sheet 12 – Choose your own collective nouns provides an extension activity that can be given to more able pupils.

Introduce the group to the idea that you can make up collective nouns for people who do different jobs by showing them the poem 'Workers' collectives'. Discuss how the invented nouns are appropriate to the jobs the people do. Ask the children to suggest other collective nouns for the various groups, e.g. a polish of cleaners, a filling of dentists, a recipe of chefs.

Workers' collectives

A brush of cleaners
A drill of dentists
A suit of tailors
A meal of chefs
A forest of carpenters
A kneading of bakers
A shower of plumbers
A parcel of postal workers.

Then give the group a copy of the activity sheet for them to complete.

Activity sheet 12 – Choose your own collective nouns

Work in a group and complete this A to Z of collective nouns for groups of workers by inventing appropriate ones. For example, a suitable collective noun for a group of auctioneers might be a bid or a lot.

A _____ of auctioneers

A _____ of bricklayers

A _____ of chemists

A _____ of doctors

A _____ of footballers

A _____ of gardeners

A _____ of hairdressers

A _____ of illustrators

A _____ of journalists

A _____ of kennel maids

A _____ of lawyers

A _____ of mechanics

A _____ of nurses

A _____ of opticians

A _____ of photographers

A _____ of quizmasters

A _____ of receptionists

A _____ of sailors

A _____ of teachers

A _____ of undertakers

A _____ of ventriloquists

A _____ of waiters

A _____ of X-ray technicians

A _____ of yachtsmen

A _____ of zookeepers

Verbs

A verb is a word which tells us what people or things are doing or being.

What is a verb?

A verb is a special kind of word.
It tells you of things being done,
Like *swim* or *talk*, *eat* or *walk*,
Creep or *crawl* or *run*.

A verb is a word that tells you
What people and things do,
Like *shine*, *sparkle*, *glow*,
Swallow, *bite* or *chew*.

Focus on verbs

Use the poem 'What is a verb?' to make sure that the pupils understand that a verb is a 'doing' word and that verbs describe actions. Point out the verbs in the poem and discuss the actions that are described.

Introduce **Activity sheet 13 –Verbs**. Discuss the nonsense poem 'Have you ever seen a drink blink?' and point out how each line in the first verse ends with a verb, which describes a thing doing something nonsensical.

Then, ask the class to complete the second verse by suggesting verbs that fill in the gaps.

Ask pairs to write another verse to add to the poem and to take it in turns to read out their poems.

Invite the pupils to re-write the paragraph about Emma Watson, changing the verbs in it. The aim of this activity is to show how important verbs are to the meaning of a sentence.

Play **Verbal Tennis**. This is a game for two players. The first person says a verb, e.g. take. The other person has to reply with another verb beginning with the second letter of that verb. In other words, a verb beginning with *a*, e.g. add. The other player then has to reply with a verb beginning with *d*, e.g. dare. The game continues until one player is unable to answer.

Activity sheet 13 – Verbs

Use verbs to complete the second verse of this nonsense poem.
Can you add a third verse which follows the same pattern?

Have you seen a drink blink?

Have you ever seen a drink blink?
No, but I've seen a fork walk.
Have you ever heard a door snore?
No, but I've heard a thistle whistle?
Have you ever seen an owl _____?
No, but I've seen a light _____
Have you ever heard a sheep _____?
No, but I've heard a fly _____

Change the Verbs

Here is a short article about Emma Watson, who played Hermione in the Harry Potter films. On your own or with one or more partners, try to replace the verbs in the article with the funniest alternatives you can think of. The first one has been done for you.

Emma Watson was born (buried) in Paris and lived (   ) in

France until she was five. Then she moved (   ) to

England, where she attended (   ) school and

learned (   ) how to sing (   ) and to

dance (   ). She had only performed (   ) in

school plays and had never acted (   ) professionally

before appearing (   ) in the Harry Potter films.

She starred (   ) in all eight films.

Language opportunities

When teaching about how instructions are written, draw attention to the verbs and how they are 'doing' words. For example, when you are teaching them how to write a recipe, before they begin to write, collect words on the whiteboard to do with cooking such as cut, peel, slice, chop, boil, cook, poach, stew, roast, simmer, fry, toast, grill, carve, sprinkle, mix, bake. Remind them what a verb is and point out that all these words are verbs.

Make copies of **Activity sheet 14 – Recipe poems**. Make sure the pupils understand that they are writing imaginary recipes, not real ones, and encourage them to be as imaginative as possible.

Activity sheet 14 – Recipe poems

Recipe for a dragon

Peel the wrinkled skin from an alligator,

Sprinkle with green dye.

Chop the wings from a vicious vulture.

Stick them firmly on the dragon's back.

Carve the claws from a tiger,

Sharpen them with a file.

Take the head from a snake,

Stir in the eyes of a tiger and the mouth of a shark.

Pour in red-hot coals from a blazing fire.

Roast in furnace for a day and a night

To make a fearsome, deadly dragon.

Talk about the poem. How do the ingredients the writer chooses help to convey the impression of a fearsome deadly dragon? List alternative ingredients that the poet might have chosen. Discuss the verbs that are used in the poem. Notice that in recipes and in other instructions the verbs are normally at the beginning of a sentence.

Write your own recipe poem. You can choose your own topic or use one of these suggestions: an alien, a sea monster, a giant, a witch.

Begin by brainstorming a list of the ingredients. Then make a list of verbs connected with cooking. As you draft your poem, refer to the two lists of ingredients and of cooking terms.

Focus on tenses

Explain that verbs are action words which have different forms or tenses, which tell you whether an action takes place in the present, the future or the past.

Write these two sentences on the board: 'Pam dives in the pool', 'Pam is diving in the pool.' Explain that in both sentences the verb is in the present tense.

Write this sentence on the board: 'Pam will dive in the pool.' Explain that the verb 'will dive' is the future tense.

Write this sentence on the board: 'Pam dived in the pool.' Explain that the verb 'dived' is in the past tense.

Remind the class what a suffix is and explain how you change the tense of many verbs simply by adding –s, –ed or –ing.

> A suffix can change the tense of a verb.
> By adding –s, –ed or –ing
> You are able to turn a verb such as walk
> Into walks, walked and walking.

Explain that, in English, a lot of words form the past tense by simply adding –ed, e.g. jumped, attacked, started, walked. However, there are a lot of exceptions, depending on how a word is formed.

Words of one syllable, with a short vowel sound, ending with a single consonant, double the consonant before adding –ed. For example: slip –slipped, tap –tapped.

There are also quite a number of words which do not add –ed, when forming the past tense. Read the poem 'Exceptional pasts' and explain that there are no rules about how the past tenses of irregular verbs are formed. Go through the poem and talk about the verbs mentioned in it which have irregular past tenses.

As an extension activity, give pupils a copy of **Activity sheet 15 – Past tenses** and ask individuals to complete it. Then ask them to swop answers with a partner and to compare whether they have given the same answers and, if not, to decide whose answer is the correct one. Then give the correct answers.

Exceptional pasts

If the past tense of ring is rung,
Shouldn't the past tense of bring be brung?
If the past tense of swim's swum or swam,
Why isn't the past tense of skim skum or skam?
If the past tense of hit is hit,
Shouldn't the past tense of sit be sit?
Surely this proves there's no sense
In how we form the past tense?

Here is a list of verbs which have an irregular past tense. Fill in the correct form of the past tense of each verb.

Verb	Past tense
begin	
bite	
bring	
choose	
drive	
fly	
forget	
give	
grow	
hit	
lay	
lead	
ride	
ring	
rise	
shake	
speak	
swim	
think	
wear	

Language opportunities

Writing recounts, such as diary entries, autobiographical narratives or reports of outings they have been on, provides good opportunities for children to focus on the past tense.

Extension activity

As an extension activity, focus on split infinitives, explaining what they are and how many writers no longer worry about whether or not they split infinitives.

Split infinitives

Explain that a split infinitive occurs when a verb is used in its infinitive form (*to walk, to consider, to go*) and an adverb is placed between the *to* and the verb, e.g. *to quickly walk, to carefully consider, to boldly go*). Splitting infinitives is traditionally regarded as incorrect usage, though many writers tend not to seriously worry if they split an infinitive.

The poem below consists of a number of split infinitives.

Split infinitives

To slowly break apart
To carelessly divide
To deliberately separate

To accidentally tear
To cruelly slice
To totally disintegrate.

Adjectives

An adjective is a word that describes or gives information about a noun.

Focus on adjectives

Use **Activity sheet 16 – Adjectives** for each pupil. Focus on the poem 'Adjectives'. Explain that an adjective describes a noun. Go through the poem pointing out the adjectives and ask the pupils to highlight them.

Ask them to underline all the adjectives in the description of 'The monster'. Then ask them individually or in pairs to rewrite the description, changing all the adjectives, so that the monster is not gruesome and fierce, but beautiful and timid.

Discuss how some adjectives describe feelings, such as *happy*, *sad*, *afraid* and *guilty*. Invite groups to make a list of adjectives which describe feelings. Encourage them to use a thesaurus, then build up a class list of adjectives which describe feelings and put it on the noticeboard.

Play the game **Act an Adjective**. You will need to prepare for this game by making a set of adjective cards, which can also be used in the game **Who's the Best?**

Act an Adjective

For this game you will need a set of adjective cards. One person from the class picks an adjective card from the pack. The person then has to go round the room behaving as though they feel like the adjective on the card, e.g. happy, sad, suspicious, fearful, hopeful, guilty and so on. The rest of the class have to guess what the adjective is. Then someone else has a turn.

Aunt Abigail's Cat is a word game in which the aim is to think of as many adjectives as you can, which start with the same letter of the alphabet.

The rules are simple. You choose a letter of the alphabet and each person in turn has to think of an adjective beginning with that letter to describe a particular animal or object. Say you've chosen the letter *a* and the chosen animal is a cat. The first person might say 'Aunt Abigail's cat is an angry cat', then the next person might say 'Aunt Abigail's cat is an active cat.' You keep going until someone can't think of an adjective beginning with *a* or suggests a word which is not an adjective.

Explain the rules and point out that any adjective will do, provided it starts with the letter *a*. It doesn't have to be one usually used to describe a cat, e.g. you could say that Aunt Abigail's cat is an awkward cat or an atrocious cat.

When you have played the game with one letter, try it with another letter, e.g. for the letter *b* think of adjectives to describe Brother Bart's boat or for *f* to describe Freddie Forest's fox.

Comparatives and Superlatives

Explain how we use adjectives to make comparisons. For example, we can say that a car is fast, but this car is faster and that car is the fastest. We add the suffix *–er* to many adjectives when we are comparing two things. This is the comparative of the adjective. We add *–est* to many words when we are comparing more than two things. This is the superlative of the adjective. Put three columns on the board labelled:

adjective	comparative	superlative
fast	faster	fastest

Ask the class for other examples to put in the columns. When good or bad is suggested, point out that some comparatives and superlatives are irregular, but add them to your list.

Who's the Best? For this game you will need a set of adjective cards. It's a game in which the class practises comparatives and superlatives. You have to choose three players at a time. The first player draws a card, e.g. loud, and uses it in a sentence, e.g. 'I've a loud voice.' The second player has to use the comparative from of the adjective e.g. 'Susie's voice is louder.' The third person has to use the superlative form, e.g. 'Majid's voice is loudest.' The game continues until the card good is drawn and the person playing the superlative says 'I'm the best.' Then the game ends or the cards are reshuffled and another game is played.

Use **Activity sheet 17 – Powerful adjectives**. Ask the children to complete the activity finding alternative adjectives. Encourage them to use a thesaurus to help them to find powerful alternatives.

Share their answers in a class discussion and write the words they suggest on the board. Words that they could have suggested include: weak – feeble, fragile, frail; fast – rapid, swift, quick; big – colossal, immense, massive; fierce – savage, ferocious, menacing; horrible – hideous, gruesome, horrific; small – tiny, minute, microscopic; evil – vile, malevolent, malicious.

Study the poem 'Choosing adjectives', pointing out the powerful adjectives that it contains. Ask the class to suggest other powerful adjectives to describe the path to the dragon's cave, the cave itself, the dragon's eyes, its breath and its teeth. List the words they suggest on the board. Ask them to suggest adjectives to describe its wings, its body, its mouth, its claws and its tail. Write them up on the board.

Ask individuals to write a description of a dragon in which they use powerful adjectives. Get them to choose words from those you have written on the board to help them with their descriptions.

Conclude the session by getting some of them to share their descriptions with the rest of the class.

Language opportunities

When a description of a character or animal occurs in a story you are reading to a class, take the opportunity that arises to focus on the adjectives that the author chooses to describe not only their appearance but also their characteristics.

Similarly, when discussing any of the characters in a story, ask the children to think of appropriate adjectives to describe that person.

When teaching about persuasive language, you can focus on the language of advertisements and how people use adjectives to describe their products and make them seem attractive. For example, a study of holiday brochures with their descriptions of 'superb' restaurants, 'fabulous' beaches and 'excellent' entertainment can be followed by pupils writing their own descriptions in which they use similar adjectives to advertise an imaginary holiday resort.

Activity sheet 16 – Adjectives

Adjectives

An adjective describes a noun,
For example, its colour: blue or brown.
It can show a size – huge, great, small;
Or tell a length – long, short or tall.
It can describe a shape – round or flat,
Wide or narrow, or thin or fat.

Adjectives describe other features too,
Whether things are ancient, old or new;
Whether a person's strong or brave;
How they look – cheerful, sad or grave.
An adjective is a describing word,
Like weird, ridiculous or absurd.

The Monster

Underline all the adjectives in this description of a monster. Then rewrite the description changing all the adjectives, so that the monster is not gruesome and fierce, but beautiful and timid. Begin 'The pretty monster raised its beautiful head...'

'The gruesome monster raised its hideous head and gave a savage snarl. It shook its immense body and its fierce red eyes shone as it opened its vicious jaws, showing its sharp teeth. It let out a tremendous roar and lashed its long, spiky tail.'

Here are ten commonly used adjectives. Suggest powerful adjectives that you could use instead of them. The first one has been done for you.

1. odd   strange, weird, bizarre

2. weak   _____

3. fast   _____

4. big   _____

5. fierce   _____

6. angry   _____

7. horrible   _____

8. small   _____

9. evil   _____

10. dark   _____

Choosing adjectives

It's a good idea always to choose
The most powerful word you can use.
Is the dragon's cave dingy and deep?
Is the path to it winding and steep?
Are the dragon's eyes fiery and bloodshot?
Is the dragon's breath scorching and hot?
Are the dragon's teeth jagged and vicious?
Is the dragon evil and malicious?

Pick out the powerful adjectives which are used in this poem and write a paragraph in which you describe a dragon, choosing powerful adjectives to make your description as vivid as you can.

Adverbs

An adverb is any word which adds to the meaning of a verb, adjective or other adverb by telling *how, why, when* or *where* an action takes place.

Focus on adverbs

Put this short verse on the board and explain that adverbs are used to give us additional information about how, why, when and where something happened.

> Adverbs tell how an action is done,
> How *slowly* or how *fast* we run.
> They tell us when events take place.
> *Yesterday* we had a race.
> They can also tell us where.
> The start was *here*; the finish *there*.

Explain that many adverbs are formed by adding *–ly* to an adjective. Either put a copy of the poem 'Adverbially speaking' on the board or give copies to groups. Write up the eight missing words – *gently furiously politely proudly idly softly lazily clearly* – and ask them to decide where they fit into the poem.

The answers are: 1 softly 2 proudly 3 lazily 4 clearly 5 gently 6 idly 7 furiously 8 politely.

Adverbially speaking

Murmuring (1) shouting loudly,
Asking anxiously, stating (2),
Nattering noisily, chattering (3),
Explaining (4), muttering crazily,
Uttering quietly, whispering (5),
Chatting (6), gossiping intently,
Talking seriously, arguing (7),
Requesting (8), enquiring curiously.

Prepare two sets of cards, one with verbs and the other with adverbs written on them. Play a game of **Which Word?** Shuffle each set of cards and ask one person to take a verb card and an adverb card. That person then has to tell a story in which the verb and the adverb are both used. The other children have to guess what the words are. The stories can be as ridiculous as the children like. Help any of them who may have difficulty starting their story by giving them a starter sentence such as 'I was running quickly down the road' or 'I woke up suddenly.'

Play the **Act an Adverb** game.

Use **Activity sheet 18 – Adverbs**. Remind the children what a pun is, then ask them to complete the activity. The answers are: 1 firmly 2 bitterly 3 sternly 4 angrily 5 thoughtfully 6 bluntly 7 patiently 8 uncertainly 9 guiltily 10 craftily.

Activity sheet 18 – Adverbs

Complete these sentences by using an adverb which makes a pun from the list at the bottom of the page.

1. 'I've been waiting an hour to see the doctor', said Tom _____

2. 'I don't like lemons', said Tom _____

3. 'It's at the back of the boat', said Tom _____

4. 'You're making me cross', said Tom _____

5. 'I've got an idea', said Tom _____

6. 'These clippers need sharpening', said Tom _____

7. 'It's no business of mine', said Tom _____

8. 'I'm not sure whether we're allowed', said Tom _____

9. 'You've caught me red-handed', Tom said _____

10. 'I'll make you a model', said Tom _____

thoughtfully   angrily   craftily   bitterly   uncertainly   firmly   guiltily
patiently   sternly   bluntly

The Act an Adverb Game

This is a game for groups of four or more. One person goes out of the room. While she is outside, the others choose an adverb. The person is invited back into the room and has to guess the adverb by asking the other players to perform actions in the way the adverb describes.
For example, if the chosen word is suspiciously, and the person asks someone to open the door then that person has to act out opening the door suspiciously. The aim of the game is not to try to trick the person who is guessing, but to help to get the correct answer as quickly as possible.

Pronouns

A pronoun is a type of word that is used in a sentence in place of a noun or noun phrase.

Focus on pronouns

Explain what a pronoun is and list examples on the board. Discuss how a pronoun enables the speaker or writer to avoid repetitions that would make what they are saying or writing long-winded.

Put this poem on the board.

> A pronoun is a kind of word,
> such as *he*, *his* and *himself*,
> that helps *you* when *you* write
> to avoid repeating *yourself*.
>
> So don't write 'Mr Smith
> was hit on Mr Smith's head.'
> Use *he* and *his* and write
> '*He* was hit on *his* head', instead.

Put the following passage on the board and start to read it aloud very slowly. Ask the class to shout out 'Stop' every time you reach a pronoun and use a marker pen to highlight the pronouns in the passage.

> 'We were sitting in our classroom and Miss was teaching us about the Romans and the clothes they wore. Trevor and I were amusing ourselves playing noughts and crosses, when he suddenly fell off his chair. All of us started to laugh, except Miss, who came storming down the room with a look of anger on her face. "Right, you two", she said, "I've had enough of your bad behaviour. You can stay in at playtime."'

Play **Pronoun Happy Families**. Explain that pronouns can be divided into seven families. Divide the children into groups of four. Ask them to write the twenty-nine pronouns onto a set of blank playing cards.

Singular pronoun families

My family: I me my mine myself

Your family: you your yours
yourselves

His family: he him his himself

Her family: she her hers herself

Its family: it its itself

Plural pronoun families

Our family: we us our ours ourselves

Their family: they them their theirs
themselves

When the cards are ready, shuffle them and deal them out equally so that three players have seven cards and the youngest player has eight cards. The aim of the game is to collect complete sets of families.

Take it in turns to ask another player for a particular card. For example: Susie, have you got 'us' from the 'we' family? If Susie has got that card, she hands it over and the person has another turn. If Susie hasn't got the card, she says 'No' and it is the next person's turn. When someone gets a whole family, she puts it down. The person who collects the most families is the winner.

Before the groups start to play the game, put the details of all the seven families on the board so that they can refer to them while they are playing the game.

Conjunctions

A conjunction is a linking word that is used to join words, phrases or clauses within a sentence. Conjunctions can also be used to join sentences together.

Focus on conjunctions

Prepare for the lesson by making cards with the following conjunctions on them: *after and although as because before but for if or since so then though unless until when while yet.*

Explain what a conjunction is and write examples of common conjunctions on the board: *and but or then because since while when although unless until.*

Put the poem 'The function of conjunctions' on the computer and put it on the whiteboard verse by verse. Point out that all the conjunctions are in italics and discuss how conjunctions can be used to join single words, phrases and clauses.

The function of conjunctions

Joining parts of sentences is the function
Of a word that is called a conjunction.

Conjunctions join one word to another:
Uncle *and* aunt, sister *and* brother.
Stop *and* think, safely *and* securely,
Rightly *or* wrongly, slowly *but* surely.

Conjunctions can link phrases too:
A complete surprise *and* out of the blue,
Once *and* for all, *but* never again
On a regular basis *or* now *and* then.

Conjunctions can join a clause with a clause:
Then we shook with fear, *when* it opened its jaws.
Because the ball hit the net, the crowd roared.
If he wasn't offside, *then* they would have scored.

Joining parts of sentences is the function
Of a word that is called a conjunction.

Hand out the conjunction cards at random and play the conjunctions game. When all the conjunctions have been used, you can collect the cards in, redistribute them and play another game.

The Conjunctions Game

The aim of the game is to practise using conjunctions by building up a story. Hand out the conjunction cards you prepared beforehand. Sit the class in a circle with all the people holding cards next to one another. Explain that you are going to build up a story in which conjunctions are used to join the phrases and sentences in the story. The story need not make complete sense, but the person whose turn it is must use their conjunction before passing the story on to the next person. The teacher will start the story and then the first person must continue it and use their conjunction before passing it on.

Here's the start of such a story:

TEACHER: I was going to the park...

PUPIL 1: (with the conjunction 'since' on the card) since I wanted to see the dragon....

PUPIL 2: (with the conjunction 'but' on their card) but it was dark...

You can start the story any way you like or use one of these examples: 'The explorer stood at the tunnel entrance...', 'The huge waves reared above the ship...', 'She came racing around the corner...'

Prepositions

A preposition is a word used before a noun or pronoun to make a phrase to do with either a place (at home), a time (before lunch), a position (inside the bag) or a way of doing something (by train).

Focus on prepositions

Explain what a preposition is and how it is used. Many prepositions are short words such as: *above after at before behind by for from in off on out since through to under up with*.

Put the poem 'The castle on the hill' on the computer and make copies of it. Put a copy on the board and read it to the class. Point out that each line begins with a preposition which refers to a place. Discuss the situation that is described in the poem and how it builds up to a sinister ending by suggesting that the young girl is a prisoner in the tower.

Give groups copies of the poem and ask them to prepare a group reading of it. Point out that they must decide which lines are going to be spoken by individuals, which by pairs and which by the group as a whole. The aim of their reading should be to make the poem sound as sinister as possible. Ask groups to practise their readings and then invite them to present them to the rest of the class.

The castle on the hill
On the hill there stands a castle.
Round the castle there is a moat.
Over the moat there is a bridge.
Beyond the bridge there is a door.
Through the door there is a courtyard.
Across the courtyard stands a tower.
Inside the tower there is a staircase.
Up the staircase there is a door.
Across the door iron bolts are drawn.
Behind the door a young girl sleeps…

Play the game **Find the Coin**.

Find the Coin

Choose someone to be the searcher and send them out of the room. While they are out of the room, hide a coin somewhere in the room. Then invite the searcher back into the room. They have to find the coin by asking questions. Each of the questions must contain a preposition. E.g. Is it near the door? Is it under a chair? Is it inside a desk? Is it below a book? If the person is stuck, the other members of the class can give them a clue, which uses a preposition, e.g. It is beneath a chair. It is near Sophie. Once the searcher has found where the coin is, choose another person to be the searcher.

Invite the children to complete **Activity sheet 19 – Space prepositions** in pairs.

Extension activity

Invite groups of more able pupils to do the **Preposition Challenge**.

You can end the focus on prepositions by explaining that some people think that it is wrong to end a sentence with a preposition. Because a Latin sentence could not end in a preposition, it used to be thought by scholars that no English sentence should end with one either. Now the rule is largely ignored.

Winston Churchill ridiculed the rule by saying: 'This is the sort of humour up with which I shall not put', which is much more awkward to say than 'This is the sort of humour I shall not put up with.'

It has, therefore, been suggested that a better rule to follow is to place the preposition where it sounds more natural. Compare the question 'What are you looking at?' with the alternative 'At what are you looking?'

Preposition Challenge

This is a game for any number of players. The aim is to compose a sentence containing as many prepositions as possible. There is no set time limit. The winner is the person whose sentence contains the most prepositions. You can if you wish start the game by getting everyone who is playing to work together to draw up a list of prepositions to which everyone taking part can refer, while they are drafting their sentence.

Here is a sentence drafted by the winner of a previous game:

> 'On Friday, at school during the morning after break, I was sitting near the front beside my friend, when from inside my lunch-box, which was under the table by the door, came the sound of tapping against the lid and the box started to slide across the floor.'

Activity sheet 19 – Position prepositions

The symbols on this sheet represent prepositions that indicate positions: across, into, off, among, down, under, through, next to, over, up, near, out, on, inside, on top of, outside, round, in, behind, above, in front of, beyond.

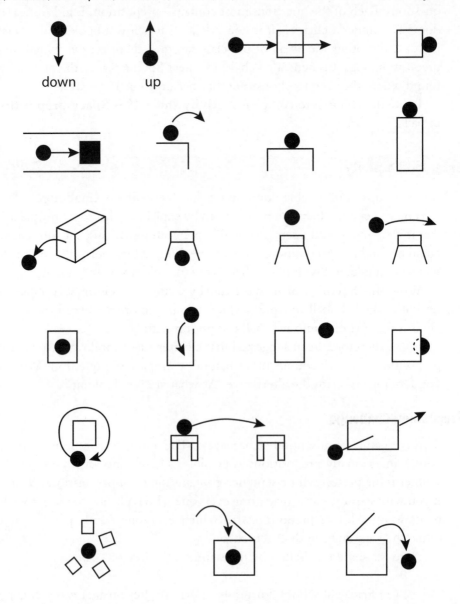

down   up

Match the symbols to the words they represent. The first two have been done for you.

Activity sheet 19 – Position prepositions answers

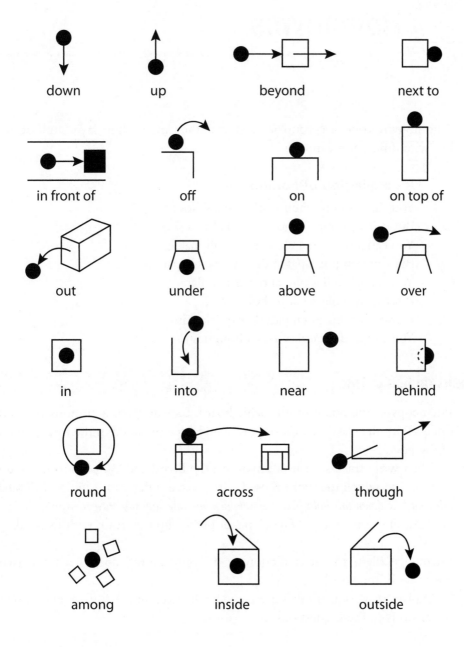

Homonyms

H is for...

A homonym is one of a group of words with the same spelling or pronunciation, but with different meanings.

> **It's a question of homonyms**
>
> You can trip up when you're on a school trip.
> But can you skip school if you fall in a skip?
> You can strike a match at a football match.
> But can you put a patch on a vegetable patch?
> You can get a flat tyre and live in a flat.
> But can you get a bat to hold a bat?
> If you give this poem another quick skim
> You can understand what's a homonym.

Focus on homonyms

Put a copy of the poem on the whiteboard. Explain what a homonym is and discuss with the class the homonyms, which are contained in the first six lines of the poem.

Then write this list of homonyms on the board and ask pairs to make up sentences in which the word is used with its two different meanings: *ball band bill boot box down fair hold horn keep light pants rose saw shy stick tie trunk.*

Give an example, e.g. 'The elephant picked up the trunk with its trunk.'

Encourage them to use a dictionary if necessary to check what the two meanings of the word are.

Explain that a lot of jokes are based on homonyms. Ask if anyone knows the answers to these questions.

1. Why did the cross-eyed teacher resign?

2. Where do fish put their money to keep it safe?

3. How do you communicate with a fish?

4. Why couldn't the music teacher open the piano?

5. Why did Frankenstein squeeze his girlfriend to death?

The answers are: 1. Because he couldn't control his pupils. 2. In river banks. 3. By dropping it a line. 4. Because all the keys were inside. 5. Because he had a crush on her.

Extension activity

Invite the children to play the game **Double Meanings**.

Double Meanings

This is a game for two or more pairs. Each pair begins by making a list of ten or more homonyms. The first pair then chooses one of the words from their list and gives its two definitions. The other pair has to guess what the word is. They score 3 points if they guess right first time, 2 if the second is right and 1 thereafter. If they have to give up, the first pair score 3 points. The pairs take it in turns to give the definitions.

Example: Say a pair choose swallow. They might say: 'We're thinking of a word that means a bird or what you do after chewing something.' The other pair guess swallow and get 3 points.

You can conclude the lesson by explaining that there are a few words which have exactly the same spelling and pronunciation but which have two opposite meanings. These include:

clip meaning join together and clip meaning to divide into two or more pieces

left meaning gone away and left meaning remaining behind

mad meaning angry about and mad being attracted to

Language opportunities

You can ask the class to bring in joke books and to find jokes which are based on homonyms. They can write or print them out and you can stick them onto a large piece of paper for display on the classroom wall.

Homophones

A homophone is one of a group of words which sound the same but which have different meanings or spellings. For example, paw and pour are homophones. So are to, too and two.

Focus on homophones

Put a copy of the poem 'The homophone blues' on the board. Ask the pupils to pick out the homophones and to highlight them. Then ask them to give other examples of homophones and list them on the board. If they are stuck, use the words from this list to prompt them: *board feet foul groan here hole pale pain piece right wait.*

The homophone blues
I woke up this morning
With the homophone blues.
I didn't know the difference
Between chews and choose.

I didn't know the difference
Between side and sighed.
I didn't know the difference
Between dyed and died.

I didn't know the difference
Between soul and sole.
I didn't know the difference
Between whole and hole.

I woke up this morning.
I was so confused.
I woke up this morning
With the homophone blues.

Make copies of **Activity sheet 20 – Homophones (1)** for each of the class to complete. It contains ten of the most common homophones which are frequently misspelled.

When they have finished, conclude the lesson by going through the list on the board, focusing on the different meanings and spellings. You can ask them to make up sentences in which the two homophones occur. For example, 'John was bored with playing board games.'

Extension activities

Use **Activity sheet 21 – Homophones (2)**. Ask the pupils to read the poem 'Spellbound' and to find the fifteen mistakes in it.

Give them a large sheet of paper. Explain that lots of jokes are based on homophones. Read the examples given on the sheet, then get them to look at joke books to find jokes based on homophones, to write the jokes onto the sheet of paper and to put the sheet of jokes on display so the rest of the class can read them.

Here are ten sets of the most common homophones. Can you fit them into the sentences correctly.

hear/here

    1. I woke up to _____ my brother shouting, 'They've arrived. They're _____.'

knew/new

    2. Although he was _____ to the class, he _____ exactly what he should do.

threw/through

    3. He _____ the ball so hard that it bounced and went _____ the window.

know/no

    4. There was _____ way that she could _____ whether the bridge was safe to cross.

past/passed

    5. He _____ the ball into the penalty area, but the centre forward's shot went _____ the post.

which/witch

    6. The _____ cackled when the wizard told her _____ spell he was going to use.

right/write

    7. It's not _____ to sell something that's broken, I'm going to _____ and complain.

wood/would

    8. She _____ not go into the _____ because the trees were so thick.

wear/where

    9. She was unsure what to _____, because she did not know _____ they were going.

their/there

    10. When they get _____, they should put _____ tickets in the machine.

Activity sheet 21 – Homophones (2)

Spellcheckers can be useful when you are writing something on a computer. But they can be misleading when a word you misspell is one of a pair of homophones.

Spellbound

I have a spelling chequer
It came with my PC
It plainly marks four my revue
Miss takes I cannot sea.
I've run this poem threw it
I'm shore your pleased too no;
Its letter perfect in it's weigh
My chequer tolled me sew.

Norman Vandal

The poem is full of mistakes. In fact, there are fifteen. Can you find them all?

Jokes

Many jokes are based on homophones. For example:

What happened when the frog left its car on a double yellow line?
It was toad away.

How did the patient get to the doctor so quickly?
He flu.

Did you hear the joke about cornflakes?
I'll tell you next week, it's a cereal.

Make a collection of jokes that are based on homophones.

Idioms

An idiom is a phrase which has a meaning that speakers of a language can understand, although the meaning is often different from what the words normally mean. In other words, it is a phrase with an actual meaning which is different from its literal meaning. For example, the idiomatic expression 'to be in hot water' means to be in trouble.

Focus on idioms

Explain what an idiom is. Put the poem 'Blowing hot and cold' up on the whiteboard and discuss how the first line of each question contains what the idiom would mean if it meant what it actually says and how the second line contains its idiomatic meaning. Point out that the title 'Blowing hot and cold' is also an idiom meaning showing mixed feelings about something, being enthusiastic, 'hot', about something, then less enthusiastic, 'cold', about it.

Blowing hot and cold

Are you in hot water when taking a bath
Or does it spell trouble for you?

Do you get hot under the collar in sunshine
And filled with annoyance too?

Will pouring cold water put out a fire
Or pour scorn on an idea?

Do you get cold feet without any socks
Or from opting out due to fear?

Ask the children to complete the matching activity on **Activity sheet 22 – Idioms (1)**

Extension activity

Make copies of **Activity sheet 23 – Idioms (2)** for more able pupils. Explain that Shakespeare added more phrases to the English language than anyone else and ask them to complete the worksheet. The answers are as follows:

1 an inevitable result, 2 in a single action, 3 the time at which something is due to be done, 4 in a chaotic mess, in a difficult position, 5 to keep out of sight, to bide one's time, 6 to take what's due or owed to you, down to the last little bit, 7 the time when one is young and inexperienced, 8 to give brief and unsympathetic consideration to something, to deal with quickly, 9 to disappear completely, 10 to take part in a useless search.

Language opportunity

When you are doing work on Shakespeare, you can talk about what an idiom is and give more able pupils **Activity sheet 23 – Idioms (2)** to complete.

There are a large number of idiomatic expressions that are connected with animals.

Match these idioms with their meanings. The first one has been done for you.

Idiom	Meaning
to talk the hind leg off a donkey	to gloat
to chicken out	to work hard
to let the cat out of the bag	to enjoy oneself thoroughly
to be the cat's whiskers	to make persistent demands
to have a whale of a time	to look embarrassed and guilty
to beaver away	to say something that is meant to be a secret
to badger someone	to talk endlessly
to look sheepish	to be the very best
to crow over something	to be cowardly and not join in

Here are some sentences containing animal idioms. Write what they mean in the space provided.

It's raining cats and dogs. _____

He took the lion's share. _____

It was like water off a duck's back. _____

He made an ass of himself. _____

He made a monkey out of me. _____

Activity sheet 23 – Idioms (2)

Shakespeare added more phrases to the English language than anyone else. Here are ten of the phrases that he added. Explain what each of them means. Their meanings are given at the foot of the page.

Phrase   *Meaning*

1. a foregone conclusion   _____

2. at one fell swoop   _____

3. high time   _____

4. in a pickle   _____

5. lie low   _____

6. pound of flesh   _____

7. salad days   _____

8. short shrift   _____

9. vanish into thin air   _____

10. a wild-goose chase   _____

© 2012, *Learning about Language: Activities for the Primary Classroom*, John Foster, Routledge

Jargon

Jargon is the term for the specialist technical language used by a particular group, e.g. by people who do the same job or who are involved in the same activity, such as a sport or hobby.

Focus on jargon

Explain what jargon means and give an example of how people use jargon in the sports they play; for example, a tennis player might challenge a decision to call the ball out at set point in a tie-break.

Test the class's knowledge of sports jargon with this quick quiz. When giving the answers point out that the advantage of using jargon is that it enables you to avoid having to make long-winded explanations by using precise technical terms instead.

Sports Jargon Quiz

1. What is a bunker in golf?
2. What is a let in tennis?
3. What is a cue in snooker?
4. What is a duck in cricket?
5. What is a nutmeg in football?
6. What is a southpaw in boxing?
7. What is a black belt in judo?
8. What is pole position in motor racing?
9. What is a try in rugby?
10. What is a jack in bowls?

(Answers: 1 a sand-filled obstacle on a golf course, 2 a ball that is served which hits the net but lands inside the service area, 3 a long tapered piece of wood or plastic used to hit the white ball across the table, 4 when a person is out before scoring a run, he makes a duck, 5 when the ball is passed through the legs of a player, 6 a boxer who leads with his left hand, 7 an expert in judo who has reached the highest level, 8 the leading position taken by the fastest car at the start of the race, 9 when the ball is touched down over the line known as the try line and points are scored, 10 the small white ball which the bowlers try to get nearest to).

Invite individuals or pairs to prepare a Jargonbusters guide to a sport or hobby, consisting of a list of terms used in that particular sport together with their meanings.

Explain that when a movie is being filmed, the film-makers have their own jargon. Put this sentence on the board: '"That's a wrap!", said the director to the gaffer.' Discuss what it means. 'That's a wrap!' means 'We've finished filming.' The director is the person in charge of what is filmed and the gaffer is the electrician in charge of lighting.

Invite them to show how much they know about movie jargon by completing **Activity sheet 24 – Movie jargon** in pairs. Encourage them to use dictionaries to help them find answers they are unsure about. The correct answers are: action b, clip a, close up b, cut a, extra b, props b, roll b, set b, shot b, take b.

Language opportunities

As part of an IT project you could invite the children to prepare a Beginner's Guide to Tech Talk explaining the technical jargon used when talking about using PCs. First, they need to list all the terms they are going to include and then to write definitions of them. Encourage them to put the words in alphabetical order and to use dictionaries to check the accuracy of the definitions they give and to look up how a dictionary defines a term which they are having difficulty defining.

Test your knowledge of the jargon used by film-makers. What do these movie terms mean? Put a tick beside the correct meaning of the word.

Action	(a) a movement made by an actor while someone else is speaking (b) what the director shouts when filming begins
Clip	(a) a small part of a film (b) an extract from the script of a film
Close up	(a) the decision to end filming for the day (b) a picture taken close to a person, for example of their face
Cut	(a) what the director says when he wants to stop filming (b) an unplanned break in filming
Extra	(a) an additional shot taken in case it is needed (b) a person other than the main actors required, for example, in crowd scenes
Props	(a) all the equipment, such as cameras, lights etc required for filming (b) all the objects that need to be on the set during filming
Roll	(a) when a camera moves position (b) when a camera is switched on and filming
Set	(a) the sequence of shots in a film (b) the place, including any scenery, where the action is being filmed
Shot	(a) an attempt at a filming a scene (b) a picture taken from a particular angle or distance
Take	(a) what the director shouts when it's time to take a break from filming (b) when a scene is actually being filmed and recorded

Kennings

A kenning is a descriptive phrase or compound word used to name something instead of a noun. It can consist of two nouns such as 'sky-candle' for the sun or of a noun plus a verb, such as 'boneshaker' for an old bicycle.

Focus on kennings

Explain what a kenning is. Talk about the origin of kennings and how Anglo-Saxon poets used them in poems, the most famous of which, Beowulf, tells the story of how the hero Beowulf slew the monster Grendel. Beowulf contains over 1,000 kennings.

Give the pupils examples of 'sky-candle' for sun and of 'whale-road' for sea. Then either give them a quiz in which you ask them to write down what they think these kennings mean or write the kennings up on the board one by one and get them to suggest what they mean

1. wave's steed   ship
2. tree-breaker   wind
3. fish-realm   sea
4. swan-road   river
5. spear-crash   battle

Explain that poets sometimes write poems called kennings, which consist of a list of such expressions about a single subject. Put the examples of 'Book' and 'Car' on the whiteboard. Discuss which poem they prefer. Ask them to pick out the phrases which most capture the nature of a book and a car. Which are the two lines that are most descriptive?

Model how to write a kennings poem by drafting one on the whiteboard. Choose a subject e.g. a dancer and brainstorm kennings which describe the person dancing.

Here is a list of kennings that one class brainstormed about a dancer:

hip-swinging	finger-pointing	leg-shaking
arm-waving	head-jerking	wrist-flapping
foot-tapping	hand-clapping	back-slapping
head-spinning	body-locking	

Draft the poem by putting the kennings they have brainstormed into an appropriate order. Here is the kennings poem that the class drafted about a dancer:

Hip-swinging
Toe-tapping
Leg-shaking
Finger-snapping

Arms-waving
Handclapper
Body-twisting
Elbow-flapper

Heel-toeing
Chicken-walking
Head-jerking
Body-talking

Give out copies of **Activity sheet 25 – Kennings** and ask individuals to write their own kennings.

Activity sheet 25 – Kennings

Book	**Car**
Page-turning	Motorway-speeding
Tale-telling	Journey-taker
Spellbinder.	Gas-guzzling
	Fume-maker.
Plot-hatching	
Cliffhanging	Gear-changing
Suspense-spinner.	Overtaker
	Tyre-squealing
Spine-shivering	Swift-braker.
Thrill-chilling	
Mystery-twister.	Slow-moving
	Traffic-queuer
Mind-bending	Non-stopping
Surprise-ending	Drive-througher.
Story-weaver.	
	Lorry-passing
	Mover-and-shaker
	Caravan-pulling
	Take-a-breaker.

Discuss the two poems. Which poem do you prefer? Pick out the phrases which most capture the nature of a book and a car. Which two lines are the most effective in each poem?

Write a kenning of your own about a boat, a train, a plane or a motor-cycle or about the moon, a hurricane, the sea or fire. Begin by brainstorming words and ideas about your chosen subject, then draft your kennings poem.

Limericks

A limerick is a humorous five-line poem with a particular pattern, first made popular by the nineteenth-century poet Edward Lear.

Lines 1 and 2 are longer lines that end with a rhyme.
Lines 3 and 4 are shorter lines that end with a different rhyme.
Line 5 is another longer line which rhymes with lines 1 and 2.

Focus on limericks

Prepare for the lessons on limericks by having a scrapbook into which they can stick limericks. Explain what a limerick is and ask the class if they know any limericks. Tell them that you are going to make a class book of limericks and invite them to recite any limericks they know and to search for limericks in the poetry books which are in the class and school libraries and any poetry books they have at home.

Examples of limericks can be found in *The Works* compiled by Paul Cookson (Macmillan) and *The Works 8* compiled by John Foster (Macmillan).

They can then type the limericks onto the computer, together with the limericks they write themselves. Make sure they put the author's name beneath each poem. Remind them what 'anonymous' means and ask them to put 'anonymous' if they do not know the author's name. Encourage them to illustrate the limericks and to make the scrapbook into a real book, with a title page, a contents page and indexes of authors, titles and first lines.

Put some examples of limericks on the whiteboard. Two examples are given below. Explain the five-line structure of the limerick (see the definition above) and point out how the last line is a punch-line – a final line which gives the verse its humour.

A young man called Rice

There was a young man called Rice
Who lived on a diet of mice.
He'd roast them or stew them,
Then crunch them or chew them.
But his breath did not smell very nice.

A young man called Paul

There was a young man called Paul,
Who went to a fancy dress ball.
He thought it would be fun
To go dressed as a bun,
But a dog ate him up in the hall.

Draft a class limerick on the whiteboard. Choose a first name such as Kate and write the first line: 'There was a young girl called Kate.' Then brainstorm words that rhyme with Kate, e.g. ate, date, fate, late, state, straight, wait. After they have come up with an initial list, encourage them to go through the alphabet to think of words they may have missed, e.g. bait, crate. Encourage them also to think of two, three and four syllable words that rhyme with Kate. There are a huge number of such words such as educate, demonstrate, exaggerate.

Invite them in pairs to draft a second line, then put some of their second lines on the whiteboard. Choose one of their suggestions as the second line. Next, ask the pairs to see if they can come up with lines 3 and 4, reminding them that these lines usually have a different rhyme from lines 1 and 2. Put some of their suggestions on the board and then, as a class, see if you can make a complete limerick by suggesting a punch-line to end the limerick.

Make copies of **Activity sheet 26 – Limericks** and ask the pupils to complete them by writing their own limericks. Encourage them to use a rhyming dictionary, such as the Oxford Junior Rhyming Dictionary, if they are stuck for a rhyme. If this doesn't help, then encourage them to rewrite the problem lines, so that other words, with a different rhyme sound, come at the end of the lines which need to rhyme.

Extension activity

Play **Consequence Limericks.** Explain that it is a game for five people and give out pencils and paper.

1. Each group has to choose five names from this list: Rose June Joan Jay Clair Marie Sue Jean Sam Ted.

2. Together they make separate lists of all the words they can think of which rhyme with the names they have chosen.

3. Each take one of the names. Sit in a circle and start by each writing the first line of a limerick on a piece of paper, using the name you have been given.

4. Without folding the paper pass it on to the person on your left.

5. The next person adds the second line to the limerick and passes it on again, for someone to write the next line. (Refer to the lists of words you made to help you to draft lines 2 and 5.)

6. Then you read out the limericks and decide which is the best.

Students can use the internet to research the history of the limerick and to find limericks written by Edward Lear. You can then explain that why this type of verse is called a limerick is uncertain. It has been suggested that it called after a place called Limerick in Ireland, because people used to sing the refrain 'Will you come up to Limerick?' between nonsense verses at a party. However, there is no real evidence for this theory.

Activity sheet 26 – Limericks

Complete this limerick in pairs or groups.

    There was a young girl called Fay
    Who went for a ride on a sleigh

    ....

    ....

    ....

Now write some limericks of your own:

    A wizard's apprentice called Jake

    ....

    ....

    ....

    ....

    A daring young man from Torquay

    ....

    ....

    ....

    ....

    A woman whose name was Chris Cross

    ....

    ....

    ....

    ....

    A mischievous girl from Poole

    ....

    ....

    ....

    ....

M is for...

Malapropisms

A malapropism is when you mistakenly say one word, when you meant to say another, because the word you actually say sounds quite like the one you wanted.

Focus on malapropisms

Explain what a malapropism is and how it is called after Mrs Malaprop, a character in Richard Sheridan's play *The Rivals*, who was famous for mixing up words in this way.

An example of a malapropism is if someone says: 'There's something wrong with your eyes. You need to see an optimist.' What they really meant to say is: 'You need to see an optician.'

Make copies of **Activity sheet 27 – Malapropisms**. Ask pairs of pupils to complete the activities. The words in the sentences are: 1 division 2 direction 3 addict 4 detention 5 punctuality 6 evacuated 7 illusion 8 turbans 9 compliments 10 eloquent.

The words which need correcting in Iris's report are: retort/report, slumber/summer, process/progress, enthralmment/enthusiasm, conservation/concentration, understatement/understanding, diffident/different, primates/climates, product/project, tutor/Tudor, expels/excels, Algeria/algebra, menial/mental, elegant/excellent.

Activity sheet 27 – Malapropisms

Here are a number of malapropisms. What did the speakers actually mean to say?

1. The maths teacher said the class was good at long derision.
2. The driver said he was travelling in the opposite dejection.
3. My dad says that I'm a TV additive.
4. The pupil was given a contention for being cheeky.
5. Good punctuation means not to be late.
6. The building had to be evaporated because there was a fire.
7. Flying saucers are just an optical delusion.
8. Sikhs wear turbines on their heads.
9. Please accept this with my condiments.
10. She gave an elegant speech.

In pairs, highlight the malapropisms in this school report on Iris Pupil. Then, take it in turns to read out what the teacher meant to write.

Iris Pupil's School Retort for the Slumber Term	Teacher Mr Mal A. Prop
Iris has made good process this term. She has shown great enthralment and conservation, especially when faced with diffident challenges. Her work in geography shows a good understatement of diffident primates and in history she did a good product on the Tutor period. In maths, she expels at Algeria and menial arithmetic. In short, she has had an elegant term.	

Metaphors

A metaphor is an expression in which a comparison is made by describing someone or something as if it actually is something else.

Focus on metaphors

Explain that, when we use a metaphor, we create a picture or image by saying that one thing *is* another thing. For example, when describing a high wind we might say 'The wind is a wolf howling round the trees and clawing at the branches.'

To help the children understand what a metaphor is, read the two nonsensical rhymes 'The sausage' and 'The baked bean'.

The sausage

The sausage is a cunning bird
With feathers long and wavy;
It swims about the frying pan
And makes its nest in gravy.

The baked bean

The greater spotted brown baked bean's
Not quite the humble bird it seems;
It lurks beneath the soggy greens
Waiting to get you.

Work with the class to produce some other nonsensical rhymes about other foods, which are based on metaphors, e.g. the wobbly jellies that dance around in wellies, the chips who put on plays dressed in skirts of mayonnaise, or the slice of bread which blushed bright red.

Give some other examples of metaphors, e.g. 'The teacher is a hawk, perched on the desk, watching us'; 'The snow was a blanket covering the fields.'

Some pupils will have difficulty in understanding what a metaphor is. They can be given the first exercise on **Activity sheet 28 – Metaphors**, which asks them to decide which of a pair of sentences means exactly what it says and which contains a metaphor.

Explain the difference between a metaphor in which we say one thing is another thing, e.g. 'The wind is a wolf howling round the trees', and a simile in which we say that one thing is *like* another thing, e.g. 'The wind is like a wolf howling round the trees.' Ask the pupils to do the second exercise on **Activity sheet 28 – Metaphors** in which they have to decide which sentences are metaphors and which are similes.

Once they have a clear understanding of what a metaphor is, work with the class to produce a poem consisting of a series of metaphors, similar to the one on thunder (see **Activity sheet 28 – Metaphors**).

In each of the following pairs, one sentence means exactly what it says. The other contains a metaphor, which could not be strictly true. Put X beside the one which contains a metaphor.

1(a) The minutes crept slowly by.
 (b) The hands on the clock moved slowly.

2(a) The aeroplane was a huge bird rising into the sky.
 (b) The aeroplane looked huge as it rose into the sky.

3(a) The moon shone brightly that night.
 (b) The moon that night was a bright golden coin.

4(a) The spy was a statue hidden in the shadow of the doorway
 (b) The spy was invisible hidden in the doorway.

5(a) A shiver of ice ran down his back.
 (b) He shivered in the bitter cold.

In each of the following pairs, one sentence contains a simile. The other contains a metaphor. Put X beside the one that is the metaphor.

6(a) The rain drummed on the roof.
 (b) The rain was like a drum beat as it fell on the roof.

7(a) The hedgehog was a prickly ball curled in its nest.
 (b) The hedgehog was like a prickly ball curled in its nest

8(a) The snake was coiled like a spring ready to strike.
 (b) The snake was a coiled spring ready to strike.

9(a) He was as angry as a wounded lion.
 (b) He was an angry wounded lion.

10(a) The tree was a bare skeleton.
 (b) The tree was as bare as a skeleton.

Activity sheet 28 – Metaphors (continued)

Work with the class to produce a series of metaphors on a chosen subject, e.g. thunder. As necessary, prompt them with ideas. Here is a list of metaphors you could build up on the subject of thunder.

Thunder is a giant snoring.

Thunder is a rhino roaring.

Thunder is a bad-tempered giant stamping his feet.

Thunder is a clash of cymbals.

Thunder is a door slamming shut.

Thunder is a drumroll.

Thunder is the crack of a gunshot.

Thunder is a bomb exploding.

Thunder is a car backfiring.

Thunder is a pneumatic drill.

Thunder is a hammer striking an anvil.

Hold a vote to decide which five of the metaphors they produce they think are most effective. Which would be the most effective metaphor to start a poem about thunder? Which would make the most effective ending? Decide on the order of the lines and put a copy of your five-line metaphor poem on the wall.

Extension activity

Encourage more able children to write metaphor poems of their own. Give them the start of some metaphor poems. Invite them to work in pairs to complete them.

> Sleep is a heavy curtain,
> Drawing itself across the mind's eye...
>
> A ship's anchor is a monster's claw,
> Clinging to the sea's bed...
>
> Hope is a delicate feather,
> Blown by the fickle wind...
>
> Toothache is a torturer,
> Relentlessly thrusting daggers of pain...
>
> The sea is a battering-ram
> Carving caves from the cliff's face...

Ask them to write metaphor poems of their own. They can either choose their own subject or choose one from this list: jealousy, freedom, fear, a mirror, fog, fire, a lake.

Nonsense

Nonsense is any piece of writing which describes nonsensical people, events or things or uses nonsense words.

Focus on nonsense poems

Write the poem 'Jumping jeans' on the board. Point out the pattern of the poem and, together with the class, draft a similar poem, e.g. 'Talking tie'. Then ask them in pairs to draft their own poems about another piece of clothing such as a sailing shirt, a singing sock, a dancing dress or a hopping hat. Explain that you are going to make a class collection of nonsense poems and ask them to type up their finished poems and to print out copies either for display or to stick into a scrapbook.

Jumping jeans

Jumping jeans, jumping jeans
Has anyone seen my jumping jeans?
They were last seen jumping on the trampoline.
Has anyone seen my jumping jeans?

Talk about nonsense poems that they know, such as 'The owl and the pussy cat' by Edward Lear, 'The walrus and the carpenter' by Lewis Carroll and 'On the Ning, Nang, Nong' by Spike Milligan. Encourage them to find copies of their favourite nonsense poems in books and on the internet and to bring them in so that you or they can read them to the class. They can also research other nonsense poems by poets such as Edward Lear, Lewis Carroll, Ogden Nash and Spike Milligan. Print out copies of their favourites for your class anthology.

Ask the children whether they know any nonsense versions of nursery rhymes, such as 'Twinkle twinkle chocolate bar'. Put a copy on the whiteboard.

Twinkle, twinkle chocolate bar

Twinkle, twinkle chocolate bar
My dad drives a rusty car.
Push the starter.
Pull the choke.
Off he goes in a cloud of smoke.

Explain that some nonsense verses are parodies. A parody is a piece of writing which imitates the style of a verse or another piece of writing in a humorous way. Use **Activity sheet 29 – Nonsense nursery rhymes** and encourage the children to write their own nonsense nursery rhymes. Alternatively, you could work with the class and draft modern versions of traditional rhymes on the board.

Activity sheet 29 – Nonsense nursery rhymes

Here are some modern versions of traditional nursery rhymes:

See-saw my bottom is sore

See-saw my bottom is sore.
I think I need a new plaster.
I get paid a piece rate,
But I'm telling you, mate,
I cannot work any faster.

If all the sea was chocolate

If all the sea was chocolate
And all the land was cake,
We wouldn't get to sleep at night
Because we'd have toothache.

The Grand Old Count of York

The Grand Old Count of York
He had ten thousand bats.
He kept them in his wardrobe
Hanging from his cloaks and hats.
And when he went out they flew out
And when he went in they flew in
And when they were neither in nor out
They haunted his neighbours' flats.

Work in pairs to complete these nonsense nursery rhymes. If you get stuck for a rhyme, use a rhyming dictionary to help you find one.

Humpty Dumpty sat on a chair
Humpty Dumpty said, 'It's not fair...

Little Miss Flynn made a terrible din...

There was an old woman who lived in a tree...

Monday's child is slimy as a snail...

Onomatopoeia

Onomatopoeia is the term used to describe words which imitate sounds associated with their meaning, e.g. hiss, buzz, clatter.

Focus on Onomatopoeia

Put this poem up on the board and explain what onomatopoeia is.

> Are you ready? Are you ready?
> Start the fizzing and the whizzing
> Start the rapping and the clapping
> Start the humming and the drumming
> Start the snipping and the snapping
> Let's give a welcome cheer
> For onomatopoeia!

Put a copy of the poem 'Sounds in the night' on the board. Explain that it is a list poem. The onomatopoeic words have been deliberately omitted, so that the children can supply them. The missing words from the lines are 2 murmur 3 whirr 4 click 5 creak 6 whistling 7 clatter 8 rumble. If there are alternatives suggested, e.g. 'howl' instead of 'whistling' or 'roar' instead of 'rumble' then accept them and discuss with the class which word they prefer.

Point out that the poem is divided into two halves – the first half dealing with sounds inside the house, the second with sounds outside the house. Invite them to add extra lines to the poem describing other sounds and draft them on the board. Then discuss where they would fit into the poem.

Sounds in the night

Listen can you hear?

The _____ of voices in the living room.

The _____ of the washing machine.

The _____ as a light is switched off.

The _____ of next door's broken gate.

The _____ of the wind as it whirls round the house.

The _____ of footsteps along the pavement.

The _____ of traffic along the by-pass.

Give out copies of **Activity sheet 30 – Onomatopoeia**. Ask individuals to complete it.

Choose one or more of the words from the list of words at the bottom of the page to describe the sounds made by each of the following:

1. A boiling kettle
2. A bonfire
3. An electric drill
4. Dry leaves being blown by the wind
5. A bomb exploding
6. A person diving in a swimming pool
7. The waves hitting a cliff during a storm
8. A guitar being plucked
9. A car braking suddenly
10. Soldiers marching
11. Big Ben striking
12. An angry lion
13. An aeroplane flying overhead
14. A door being shut quickly
15. A washing-machine
16. A gale-force wind
17. A glass being dropped on a wooden floor
18. Two friends talking quietly
19. A firework going off
20. A parrot

bang blast boom chatter chime clang clatter crack crackle crash crunch dong drone groan growl gurgle hiss howl hum lash moan murmur peal plink plop ring roar rumble rustle scream screech slam slosh smack smash splash stamp squawk squeal swoosh thud thump thunder thrash tinkle tramp twang wail whine whirr whisper whoosh

Ask groups to make a sound collage by grouping sounds under a particular heading such as sounds of the playground, sounds of the kitchen, sounds at the fair, sounds at the seaside, sounds in the city, animal sounds. They can then cut out pictures that illustrate the sounds. The sound words can be written on strips of paper and stuck over the picture connected with that particular sound.

Invite the children to write their own list poems about sounds in a particular place, e.g. sounds of the classroom, sounds of the playground, sounds of the fair. They can begin their poems with the line 'Listen, can you hear?' Once they have finished drafting their poems, ask them to think about the order of the lines before they copy out the poem. Would putting another line first make a better beginning? Is the last line the best way of ending the poem? Ask them to indicate any changes they want to make to the order of the lines by numbering them before copying out the finished poem.

Invite the children to write a poem listing 'Ten things heard at the witches' ball', 'Ten things heard at the pirates' party' or 'Ten things heard at the dinosaurs' dance'. You can read them the poem 'Ten things heard at Hallowe'en' to use as a model.

Ten things heard at Hallowe'en

The cackle of witches' laughter
The creak of a coffin lid
The moan of a groaning ghost
The rattling bones of a skeleton
The hissing of a witch's cat.
The wail of a tormented zombie
The eerie sigh of a lost spirit
The ghastly groan of a ghoul
The midnight howl of a werewolf.
A bloodcurdling shriek.

Get the children to look through their comics and to look at cartoon books, such as the Asterix books, to find examples of onomatopoeia being used to describe unusual or amusing sounds, e.g. BRAOUM.

Invite them to imagine they are creating a cartoon strip. What new onomatopoeic words would they invent for these sounds?

someone falling head first into a pond full of slime
a giant robot falling to pieces
a boy falling into a bed of nettles
a witch's cat having its tail trodden on

Language opportunities

When working on the senses, you can introduce work on onomatopoeia in dealing with the sense of sound.

Palindromes

A palindrome is a word or phrase which reads the same backwards as it does when read forwards.

Focus on palindromes

An explanation of palindromes can be linked to work on the family and on people's names. Put a copy of 'A question of names' on the whiteboard. Explain that some names are palindromes and ask the class to pick out the palindromes in the poem.

A question of names
Why is Pip like Pop
But Bob not like Rob?
Why is Mum like Dad
But Nan not like Gran?
Why is Anna like Hannah
But Eve not like Steve?
Why is Ada like Otto
But Lil not like Jill?

Explain that there are lots of words which are palindromes. Do they know any examples? Collect examples on the whiteboard such as: pup, eye, deed, noon, toot, radar, level, kayak, refer and redder.

Discuss how some phrases and sentences are palindromes. Write some examples up on the whiteboard.

Never odd or even
Step on no pets
No lemons, no melon
Draw, O Coward!
Was it a car or a cat I saw?

Ask the class: Do they think the two well-known palindromes (below) are true or made up. Discuss why they are unlikely to be true.

'Able was I ere I saw Elba' (which the French Emperor Napoleon is reputed to have said when sent into exile on the island of Elba)

'Madam, I'm Adam' (which Adam is reputed to have said when introducing himself to Eve in the garden of Eden)

Talk about how another type of palindrome is one formed by words rather than letters. Give an example: 'You can cage a swallow, can't you, but you can't swallow a cage, can you?'

End the session by telling the children that, in the past, people believed palindromes were magical. They were carved on amulets and on walls to provide people and property with protection from harm.

Language opportunities

An explanation of what a palindrome is can be linked to work on families and names. Alternatively it can be introduced when a word which is a palindrome, such as level, radar or kayak, occurs in topic work.

Personification

Personification is a special kind of metaphor in which human qualities such as speech, feelings, actions and appearance are given to objects or other creatures.

Focus on personification

Remind the pupils what a metaphor is (see p. 92) and explain that personification is a special type of metaphor. Put the poem 'On a calm day' on the board and discuss how the wind, the leaves, the clouds and the sea are all given human characteristics.

On a calm day

On a calm day
The wind whispers softly,
The leaves in the trees dance.
Clouds amble across the sky
And the sea washes the shore,
Stroking it gently.

Point out that it is the verbs in the poem which describe human actions. Together with the class, draft a similar poem, 'On a stormy day'. Ask them to suggest alternative verbs which suggest that the wind, the leaves, the clouds and the sea are behaving as persons.

Extension activity

Give more able pupils a copy of **Activity Sheet 31 – Personification** to complete.

Giant Winter

Giant Winter preys on the earth,
Gripping with talons of ice
Squeezing, seeking a submission,
Tightening his grip like a vice.

Starved of sunlight, shivering trees
Are bent by his torturing breath.
The seeds burrow into the soil
Preparing to fight to the death.

Giant Winter sneers at their struggles,
Blows blizzards from his frozen jaws,
Ripples cold muscles of iron,
Clenches tighter his icicle claws.

Just as he seems to be winning,
Strength suddenly ebbs from his veins.
He releases his hold and collapses.
Giant Spring gently takes up the reins.

Snarling, bitter with resentment,
Winter crawls to his polar den,
Where he watches and waits till it's time
To renew the battle again.

Discuss how Winter is personified in this poem as a giant. Pick out the words and phrases which suggest Winter feels and acts like a giant human. Which verse most effectively personifies Winter?

Write a poem of your own in which you use personification to describe a natural feature such as a waterfall, a river or a volcano, fog or snow, an object such as a clock or a mirror, or a creature such as a spider, a cat or a dog.

Plurals

The word 'plural' means consisting of more than one.

Focus on plurals

Explain that the plural of most words is formed by adding either −s or −es, depending upon the last one or two letters of the word, and that there are some rules you can learn which help you to form plurals correctly.

Use the poem 'How to make plurals'. Focus on verses 1 and 2 and make sure the pupils understand the most common way of forming plurals. Ask them to think of other words that end in −s, and add −es and put them on the board (addresses, guesses, successes).

Then go on to verse 3 and explain that words ending in −x, −ch and −sh add −es when forming their plurals.

Ask groups to do the **Plurals Challenge**. Ask each group to draw three columns on a large piece of paper labelled 'Words ending in −x', 'Words ending in −ch' and 'Words ending in −sh'. Set a time limit (e.g. 15 minutes) and hold a competition to see how many plurals ending −es they can list in the three columns. Encourage them to use a rhyming dictionary to help them.

Words that they might list include: foxes, boxes, benches stenches, trenches, wenches, wrenches, inches, finches, pinches, branches, launches, haunches, lunches, hunches, punches, ashes, crashes, dashes, flashes, gashes, lashes, rashes, splashes, fishes, dishes, wishes, washes, blushes, brushes, flushes, rushes, thrushes, searches, watches, blotches, catches.

When checking their lists, ask them to use a dictionary if they want to challenge any words on other groups' lists.

Make class lists of plurals of words ending in −ch and −sh and put them on display.

Recap the rules they have learned about adding −s and −es in a follow-up session, then go on to the fourth verse too and discuss how words ending in a consonant followed by a −y change the y to an i and, therefore, add −ies to form their plurals. Make a class list of words ending in −*y* that add −*ies* to form their plurals and put it on display.

Look at verses 5 and 6 and talk about how most words ending in −*f* or −*fe* drop the −*f* or −*fe* and add −*ves*. But there are some exceptions: chiefs, proofs, roofs, beliefs.

Write this quiz on the board and either ask individuals to write answers to it or test the class orally.

Which of these pairs are wrong?

1. leaf   leaves
2. chief   chiefs
3. wolf   wolfs
4. knife   knifes
5. wife   wives
6. shelf   shelfs
7. half   halfs
8. scarf   scarfs
9. cliff   cliffs
10. life   lives
11. calf   calfs
12. elf   elves

Irregular plurals

Explain that there are some words which have irregular plurals. Can the class think of any?

Irregular plurals include: man>men woman>women child>children foot>feet mouse>mice tooth>teeth.

Discuss words which do not change at all when they are plural, such as deer and sheep.

There are also some words which are always plural, such as clothes and riches.

How to make plurals

To make most plurals you don't have to guess.
To the word you're writing just add −s,
Like tables and chairs, hats and coats,
Swans, rivers and streams and boats.

But watch out if you want success
With words already ending with —s.
In that case you add an —es
So dresses is the plural of dress.

And to words ending in —x ,—ch or —sh
Adding —es is what you must do
Making boxes and foxes, benches and branches,
And thrushes and brushes too.

For words ending with a consonant and a —y
You must change the y to an i
So you add —ies to make flies,
Mysteries, stories and spies.

When a word ends in —f or —fe
You must change it to —ve and add —s.
A calf becomes calves and a leaf becomes leaves,
But you'll find to your distress

That this rule doesn't always apply,
And the f stays the same in chiefs,
In reefs and in roofs, in dwarfs and in proofs,
And also in gulfs and beliefs.

Some words ending in —o just add —s,
So a piano becomes pianos.
But other words add an —es
Like mosquitoes and buffaloes.

There are some words that don't change at all.
Here's a short list that's just for you.
There are deer and aircraft and sheep.
Thank goodness they're only a few!

And last but not least come those words
That change in a different way.
But why mouse becomes mice and tooth becomes teeth,
I'm afraid that I really can't say.

Extension activity

Give more able pupils a copy of the poem and ask them to list the rules for making plurals that are included in it. Then invite the pupils to try to write a sentence containing an example of each of the rules for making plurals, which they have identified.

Here's an example of such a sentence: 'The girls were sitting on the benches, wearing dresses and scarves, playing tunes on their piccolos.'

Play **Plurals Bingo**. This activity requires a lot of preparation, but once the cards are made you can use them again and again. Begin by making a number of cards which have twenty-five squares on them arranged in rows of five. Write twenty-five plurals from the list below in the squares on each card, varying the words and the order in which you write them on the card. Then write the singular form of the fifty words in the list on a slip of paper each and put the slips in a large envelope. You also need counters for the pupils to use instead of putting a cross on the cards. Distribute the cards, one per group, and draw the slips one by one from the envelope. The first group which gets five plurals in a row is the winner.

List of plurals to write on the cards: dresses guesses successes addresses foxes boxes benches trenches blushes brushes thrushes lunches bunches punches inches branches bushes dishes fishes wishes ashes crashes flashes splashes mice teeth children feet sheep deer geese mosquitoes potatoes pianos glasses stories mysteries spies calves chiefs beliefs leaves loaves wolves berries ferries boundaries quarries laboratories.

Pronunciation

Pronunciation is the term used for the way people speak or pronounce words.

Focus on pronunciation

Explain that how you pronounce words depends on what accent you have. Some people have a regional accent, depending on which part of the country they come from. Many people today speak with a neutral accent and it can be hard to tell where they come from.

Discuss with the class how they pronounce certain words, e.g. bath, castle. Some people pronounce it with a short a, others with a long a. It depends where you come from.

Talk about how it can be difficult to know how to pronounce a word, because words which have the same combination of letters in them may be pronounced differently.

Explain that the letters *ough* can be pronounced in nine different ways.

Write this sentence on the board and discuss how the words with *ough* in them are pronounced differently: 'The rough-coated, dough-faced, thoughtful ploughman strode through the streets of Scarborough; after falling into a slough, he coughed and hiccoughed.'

Extension activity

Give groups of more able pupils the poem 'Hints on pronunciation for foreigners'. Ask them to discuss how words which are spelt the same are pronounced differently, e.g. tough, bough, cough, dough; heard, beard; meat, great, sweat.

Then ask them to list words which are pronounced similarly, but spelt differently, e.g. know, dough; heard, word, bird; sweat, yet; they, weigh, pray.

Hints on pronunciation for foreigners

I take it you already know
Of tough and bough and cough and dough.

Beware of heard, a dreadful word,
That looks like beard and sounds like bird.

Watch out there's meat and great and sweat.
Do you know how to say them yet?

Look out for they and weigh, and pray.
You'll learn to speak like us one day!

Study the poem and make lists of the words in each of the first three verses that are spelt the same but pronounced differently.

Verse 1	Verse 2	Verse 3

Then make lists of the words in each of the four verses that are pronounced similarly but spelt differently.

Verse 1	Verse 2	Verse 3	Verse 4

Proverbs

A proverb is a short, memorable saying which expresses a truth or a well-known fact.

Focus on proverbs

Explain what a proverb is and give some examples, such as:

A rolling stone gathers no moss.
You can lead a horse to water, but you can't make it drink.
He who hesitates is lost.
Let sleeping dogs lie.

Give out **Activity sheet 33 – Proverbs** and ask the children to complete it. The answers are 1.a 2.b 3.b 4.b 5.a 6.b 7.b 8.b 9.a 10.b.

Invite them to compile an alphabet of proverbs. Encourage them to use the internet to find examples.

Ask more able groups to tackle the extension activity, which involves either altering or adding to existing proverbs.

Extension activity

Scrambled proverbs

Explain that you can play with proverbs by either altering them or adding to them. Here are some examples:

Many hands make light work.
A lazybones will always shirk.

Many hands get dirtier than one pair.
No news means that the computer is broken.
It's no use shutting the stable door if the horse is still outside.
You can't teach an old dog the alphabet.
Every cloud has a shower in it.
All roads lead somewhere.

Early to bed, early to rise
Makes a man healthy, wealthy and wise.
Late to rise and late to bed
Makes a man lazy and grumpy instead.

You can end the session by explaining that some proverbs contradict each other. Here are some that do. Can they think of any others?

Great minds think alike.   Fools seldom differ.
Too many cooks spoil the broth.   Many hands make light work.

Activity sheet 33 – Proverbs

Complete these proverbs:

1. The early bird_____
   _____
   (a) catches the worm
   (b) sings   loudest   and   longest

2. A leopard cannot_____
   _____
   (a) become a kitten
   (b) change its spots

3. Where there's a will_____
   _____
   (a) there's no obstacle to overcome
   (b) there's a way

4. Don't put off till tomorrow _____
   _____
   (a) what should have been done
       yesterday
   (b) what you can do today

5. Revenge is _____
   _____
   (a) sweet
   (b) a bitter pill to swallow

6. Many hands _____
   _____
   (a) make agreement impossible
   (b) make light work

7. Don't cry_____
   _____
   (a) if you haven't got a handkerchief
   (b) over spilt milk

8. The last straw_____
   _____
   (a) is the shortest
   (b) breaks the camel's back

9. Don't count your chickens_____
   _____
   (a) before they are hatched
   (b) until they've crossed the road.

10. It never rains _____
    _____
    (a) where the sun shines brightest
    (b) but it pours

An alphabet of proverbs

In groups see if you can complete this alphabet of proverbs:

> **A** rolling stone gathers no moss.
> **B**eauty is in the eye of the beholder.
> **C**harity begins at home...

You may not be able to find a proverb beginning with each of the letters of the alphabet. But see which group can find the most within a set time.

Punctuation

Punctuation is the use of symbols, known as punctuation marks, in our writing to make it easier to understand.

Focus on punctuation

Explain why we have punctuation, and that punctuation marks help readers in several ways.

They indicate where one sentence ends and another begins.
They show where there is a pause in a sentence.
They show what type of sentence it is – a statement, a question or an exclamation.

Put 'What the punctuation marks said' on the whiteboard. Make large cards with full stop, comma, semicolon, colon, apostrophe, exclamation mark and question mark written on them. Explain why we have punctuation marks and what each one looks like.

Choose seven people to stand in front of the class, each holding one of the cards, but not showing which one it is. Ask the rest of the class to read out what each punctuation mark said. The person holding the appropriate card turns it over and shows the class when that punctuation mark speaks.

What the punctuation marks said

'You must stop for me,' said the full stop.
'I tell you when there is a short pause,' said the comma.
'I am stronger than a comma, but weaker than a full stop.
You will find me in longer sentences between two clauses,' said the semicolon.
'I introduce a list, a saying or a statement,' said the colon.

'You'll find me when you've missed letters out,' said the apostrophe.
'I can also show possession and that something belongs to somebody.'
'Halt! Stop! Look out! Beware! I emphasise and show feelings,' said the exclamation mark.
'I ask Who? What? When? Why? How? I expect an answer,' said the question mark.
'Don't ignore us,' chorused the punctuation marks. 'You'll lose marks if you do.'

Focus on capital letters

Explain that, when we write, we can use either capital letters or lower case letters. Put the poem 'CAPITAL LETTERS' on the whiteboard.

> We are CAPITAL LETTERS.
> Use us at the start of names
> of places like London and Glasgow,
> and people like Gopal and James.
> Use us at the start of a sentence,
> and for I, but not for you;
> to draw attention to DANGER,
> and for places like CIRCUS and ZOO.

Ask groups to list the four uses of capital letters that are explained in the poem. Discuss the uses with the class and point out that capitals are used not only at the start of names of people and places, but also for the days of the week and the months of the year.

Ask them to look at the title of the book they are reading. What do they notice about the use of capital letters? Discuss how capitals are often used for the main words in the titles of books, films or songs. Write some examples on the whiteboard, e.g. The Wizard of Oz, The Lion, the Witch and the Wardrobe, I'm Dreaming of a White Christmas.

Explain that capital letters are also used when we write a person's title. Make sure they understand what a title is and write examples on the whiteboard, e.g. Ms, Mr, Miss, Sir, Lord, etc.

Put a copy of the paragraph (below) on the whiteboard and ask the pupils to copy out the passage putting in capital letters where they have been left out.

> 'i went to the odeon cinema in oxford yesterday. we saw the last harry potter film called harry potter and the deathly hallows – part two.

afterwards i went to macdonalds and i had a big mac meal, then we caught the bus back to abingdon.'

Learning opportunities

Teaching formal letter-writing provides a good opportunity to remind pupils about the use of capital letters in the name and the title of the person to whom they are writing, in the names of places in the address, and to begin the day of the week and month of the year in the date.

When they are writing in their reading record, or writing a book review or a blurb, you can remind the children that they should use capitals for the start of the author's name, and of the main words in the book's title, and for the start of the names of any characters or places they include in their writing.

Focus on full stops

Put the poem (below) on the whiteboard. Explain that the full stop is the basic punctuation mark. It marks a long pause and must be used at the end of every sentence, except sentences which are questions (in which case a question mark is used) or exclamations (in which case an exclamation mark is used).

> A full stop must end a sentence.
> There is no doubt about it.
> In our reading and our writing
> We cannot do without it.

Put the following paragraph, from which all the full stops and capital letters have been omitted, on the whiteboard.

> 'last year my sister jodie and i went to scotland we went to stay with my aunt jean who lives in glasgow my dad drove us to oxford station we had to wait an hour because the train was late then we had to change trains at birmingham the engine broke down outside carlisle we had to wait while they brought another engine the journey to scotland took us ten hours and i got very bored'

Explain that all the capital letters and full stops in the paragraph have been missed out and that you are going to choose two people to act as the Talking Capital and the Speaking Full Stop. You are going to read the passage slowly and it is their job to tell you where to put a capital and where to put a full stop.

The rest of the class are to watch carefully and are to interrupt if the Talking Capital misses a capital or the Speaking Full Stop misses a full stop.

Make copies of **Activity Sheet 34 – Full stops**. Give it to any pupils who are still having difficulty with using full stops to end their sentences.

Ask the other pupils to focus on a recent piece of their writing. Are there any places where they have left out a full stop? In pairs, show each other their work and discuss any places where a full stop has not been used when it should have been.

Learning opportunities

When the pupils have completed a long writing task, such as a recount of a trip they have been on, invite them in pairs to look at each other's writing before it is handed in to be marked, to see if any full stops or capital letters have been missed out.

Each line has two sentences with the capital letters and full stops missing. Copy the sentences out putting in the missing full stops and capital letters. The first one has been done for you.

there once was a full stop it was lost

There once was a full stop. It was lost.

it was on its way home there was a storm

the full stop was frightened it did not know what to do

the lightning flashed the thunder crashed

the rain poured down the full stop was soaked

it was very dark the full stop could not see the path

there was a turning it did not know which way to go

the full stop started to cry it was lost

Focus on commas

The comma is the second key punctuation mark. It is used inside longer sentences in order to break the sentences up and make them easier to read.

Explain that commas are used in several different ways.

■ To separate the words in a list. The list may be:

a list of nouns, e.g. Manjit, Paolo, Louis and Sarah looked at me.
a list of adjectives, e.g. The stone was smooth, round, green and priceless.
or a list of adverbs, e.g. The fox crept silently, stealthily, slyly.

Point out that a comma is not usually put before 'and' in a list.

■ To separate a list of phrases in a sentence:

e.g. He lifted the latch, slowly pushed open the gate, waited for a moment, then sprinted across the lawn.

■ To divide off a phrase which is used in a sentence in order to add to the meaning of a word, especially a noun:

e.g. Prince Harry, a keen rugby fan, presented the trophy.

■ To separate the different parts of a complex sentence:

e.g. Before Hercules had time to reach for his sword, the huge beast, which had been lurking in the shadows, leapt out at him.

Give individuals **Activity sheet 35 – Commas** to complete.

Right or wrong?

Put a tick beside the sentences in which commas are used correctly and a cross against the sentences in which they are used incorrectly.

1. For lunch there is either soup, pizza, chicken nuggets or ham salad.
   There is a choice of apples pears bananas or plums.

2. The monster had sharp red pointed teeth.
   The monster had enormous, sharp, vicious claws.

3. The hunter moved cautiously, carefully and silently towards his prey.
   The hunted deer ran quickly anxiously, and fearfully through the forest.

4. The message which was on the table was in some sort of code.
   The hole, which he had seen at the back of the cave, was empty.

5. The girl, unsure what to do next, took a step backwards, then jumped.
   The power switch which was on the opposite wall was out of his reach.

6. The winning captain, Phil Jones, was presented with the trophy.
   The last man to leave the ship the captain was badly hurt.

7. Since there was no chance of knowing which was the right way, he went straight on, but found his way blocked by a huge pile of rubble, where the roof of the tunnel had collapsed.
   She felt under pressure, but it was up to her now because she was the eldest who the others expected to lead them to safety.

8. It was cold and dark, the only light coming from a window, which was so high up in the wall that, even standing on the stool, he was unable to reach.
   There was nowhere he could go nothing he could do except wait, hoping that someone would realise he was missing.

Focus on semicolons

Explain what a semicolon looks like and discuss how it is used inside a sentence to mark a pause that is longer than a comma, but shorter than a full stop. Talk about how it is often used in sentences which have two main clauses that are not joined by a conjunction.

Write on the board examples of sentences in which a semicolon is used.

Some people are good at maths; others are not.

Yesterday, I went fishing; today, I am going to the cinema.

England have no chance of winning; Scotland have no chance either.

Wise men learn from others mistakes; fools learn from their own.

Focus on colons

Explain what a colon is and that it has the same force as a semicolon. One of its main uses is to introduce a list. Write on the board some examples of the use of a colon.

Here's what we need to buy: a torch, some batteries, a lunchbox and a waterproof jacket.

The programme is as follows: on Monday there's swimming, on Tuesday climbing, on Wednesday we'll go for a walk, on Thursday canoeing and on Friday you go back home.

Focus on hyphens

Explain what a hyphen looks like and put the poem on the board. Talk about how a hyphen is used to join words.

Point out that the hyphen is different from a dash. Whereas a hyphen is used to join words together, a dash is used to indicate a break within a sentence.

Example: I was going to the shops – you know, the ones opposite the rec.

Explain that dashes are more often used informally in speech, as in the example above. It is better to avoid using them in formal writing.

I am a humble hyphen.
I can help you to make
New words by joining words,
For example, give-and-take.

I can make it half-term,
Make your holiday first-rate,
Take you to a drive-through,
Keep you cool and up-to-date.

Speech marks

When anyone speaks in a story, the writer uses speech marks to show which words are spoken. They look like this ' ' or this " ". Speech marks are sometimes called inverted commas.

Focus on the punctuation of speech

Explain that there are rules about the punctuation of speech and how to use speech marks. Use **Activity sheet 36 – Punctuating speech**. Explain that it is an extract from a story called 'The Silver Box' and go through the rules for punctuating speech.

Ask them to practise using speech marks by continuing the story, writing the conversation that the three children had as they looked more closely at the box and discussed what they should do with it.

Activity sheet 36 – Punctuating speech

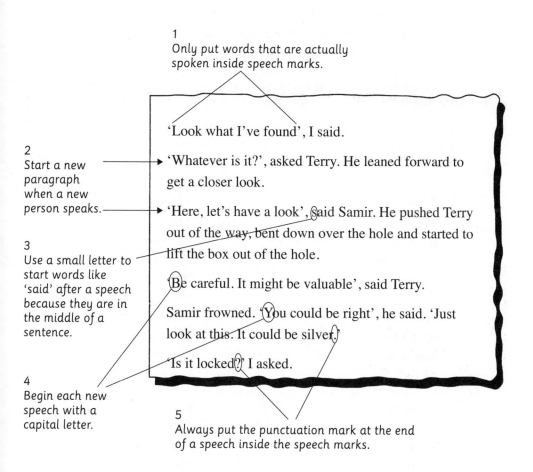

1
Only put words that are actually spoken inside speech marks.

2
Start a new paragraph when a new person speaks.

3
Use a small letter to start words like 'said' after a speech because they are in the middle of a sentence.

4
Begin each new speech with a capital letter.

5
Always put the punctuation mark at the end of a speech inside the speech marks.

'Look what I've found', I said.

'Whatever is it?', asked Terry. He leaned forward to get a closer look.

'Here, let's have a look', said Samir. He pushed Terry out of the way, bent down over the hole and started to lift the box out of the hole.

'Be careful. It might be valuable', said Terry.

Samir frowned. 'You could be right', he said. 'Just look at this. It could be silver.'

'Is it locked?' I asked.

Continue the story of the silver box. Write the conversation the children had as they looked at the box and discussed what they should do with it.

Language opportunities

There are lots of opportunities for activities on speech marks when you are reading a story with the class. For example, find an extract which involves a conversation between several people. Ask groups to read the extract together as follows: one of them takes the part of the narrator, reading everything except the words spoken, others take the parts of the various characters reading only what they actually say, and one person takes the part of the punctuation marks and reads them out whenever they appear.

Focus on apostrophes

Explain that apostrophes have two uses and that one use is to show that words have been shortened and that certain letters have been left out.

Put the two versions of the poem on the board.

That's it	**That is it**
That's it.	That is it.
It's done.	It is done.
You've lost.	You have lost.
We've won.	We have won.
Who's next?	Who is next?
I can't be.	I cannot be.
You're sure.	You are sure
it's me?	it is me?
He isn't.	He is not.
What's what?	What is what?
She's cold.	She is cold.
We're hot.	We are hot.
I'm ready.	I am ready.
Don't wait.	Do not wait.
You'll see.	You will see.
We'll be late.	We will be late.

The one with apostrophes in contains many of the most common examples of this use of the apostrophe. Split the class into two groups and ask one group – Group A – to read the shortened versions and the other group – Group B

– to read the longer versions. Read the complete poem in this way i.e. Group A: That's it. Group B: That is it. Group A: It's done. Group B: It is done and so on. Then repeat the reading with Group B reading the shortened versions and Group A reading the longer version.

Talk about *won't* and *shan't*. Explain that the shortened form of *will not* is *won't* and the shortened form of *shall not* is *shan't*. Tell them that this is because *willn't* and *shalln't* are difficult to say. Get them to make up some sentences using *won't* and *shan't* and put them on the board, with *willn't* and *shalln't* written instead of *won't* and *shan't* and invite some of them to try saying them.

Play **Apostrophe Dominoes**. You will need to prepare for this game by making twenty-eight domino cards (see p. 130).

Apostrophe Dominoes

This is a game for two players. Shuffle the cards and deal each player seven cards. Place the remaining cards face down on the table. Player 1 starts by putting down a domino. For example, say he puts down *it's ++ they will*. Player 2 must put down either *they'll* or *it is*. If player 2 cannot go, he picks up a card from the pile on the table and it is then player 1's turn again. The game goes on until one person runs out of cards, or until both people are stuck. The winner is the person with the fewest cards at the end.

Apostrophes of possession

Explain that the other use of the apostrophe is to show possession. The apostrophe tells the reader that someone (or something) belongs to someone (or something) else, e.g. *John's uncle*, *Helen's pen*, *the car's horn*, *the dog's basket*

Use **Activity sheet 37 – Apostrophes of possession** to explain what the three rules are.

Dominoes (each showing two contraction/expansion halves):

you'll	◆	I will
we're	◆	cannot
they'll	◆	are not
hadn't	◆	I have
there's	◆	you will
don't	◆	we are
it's	◆	they will
I'm	◆	had not
weren't	◆	there is
that's	◆	do not
we've	◆	it is
didn't	◆	I am
they've	◆	were not
we'll	◆	that is
won't	◆	we have
isn't	◆	did not
he'd	◆	they have
she's	◆	we will
they're	◆	will not
should've	◆	is not
she'll	◆	he had
wasn't	◆	she is
you're	◆	they are
shan't	◆	should have
I've	◆	she will
I'll	◆	was not
can't	◆	you are
aren't	◆	shall not

Activity sheet 37 – Apostrophes of possession

There are three main rules about how to use the apostrophe to show possession.

Rule 1

When the word is singular (meaning there is only one owner) you add *'s* (apostrophe s), e.g. the coat of the girl > the girl's coat.

Copy out these phrases and make them shorter by using apostrophes.

1. the house of my grandmother
2. the room of Sally
3. the purr of the cat
4. the rattle of the baby
5. the gloves of the goalkeeper
6. the study of the headteacher

Rule 2

When the word is plural (meaning there is more than one owner) and the word ends in *s* you add only an apostrophe, e.g. the bicycles of the boys > the boys' bicycles.

Copy out these phrases and make them shorter by using apostrophes.

1. the mother of the girls
2. the voices of my friends
3. the howls of the wolves
4. the branches of the trees
5. the wheels of the cars
6. the wings of the butterflies

Rule 3

When the word is plural but does not end in s you add *'s* (apostrophe s), e.g. the smiles of the children > the children's smiles.

Copy out these phrases and make them shorter by using apostrophes.

1. the hats of the men
2. the laughter of the women
3. the roars of the crowd
4. the names of the people

The *Spelling hints* below explain some of the difficulties that pupils often experience when starting to use apostrophes, because they confuse words which sound alike. These can be given to individuals when they make mistakes in their writing.

Spelling hints

Its and it's

The word *its* means 'belonging to it' and does not have an apostrophe. Neither do *hers, ours, yours* or *theirs*.

It's is the shortened form of *it is* or *it has*. So it has an apostrophe.

> If you mean it is when you say it's
> You must fit an apostrophe in it's
> But if you mean belonging to it
> Then its has no apostrophe in it.

Whose and who's

The word *whose* means 'belonging to whom' and does not have an apostrophe, whereas w*ho's* is the shortened form of *who is* and therefore has an apostrophe.

Example: 'Who's Hugh?' but 'Whose shoes are those?'

Where, wear and we're

Explain the different meanings of *where, wear* and *we're*.

> *Where* is a place in which something is situated or happening.
> Example: 'This is my bedroom where I do my homework.'

> *Wear* means to have something on your body or face.
> Example: 'I am going to wear my new T-shirt to the party.'

> *We're* is a shortened form of *we are*.
> Example: 'We're going on holiday next week.'

Give individuals a copy of this rhyme. They can use it to remind themselves of the different meanings.

> Where are you going on holiday?
> What are you going to wear?
> We're going to the seaside.
> We'll wear our swimming trunks there.

There, their and they're

Explain the different meanings of *there, their* and *they're*.

There is an adverb meaning in that place.
Example: 'I went there for my holidays.'

Their is a pronoun meaning belonging to them.
Example: 'They packed the suitcases ready for their holiday.'

They're is a shortened version of *they are*.
Example: They're going to Spain for their holiday.

Extension activities

As an extension activity with more able pupils, use the poem (below) in which all the apostrophes have been used wrongly. Can you make a copy of it with the apostrophes in the right places?

Dads views' on apostrophe's

Apostrophe's often appear in place's
where they are not mean't to,
like in grocery shop's windows'
advertising orange's and apple's,
or they are omitted where they shouldnt be.
Its all very confusing, isnt it?
Dad say's if hed got any say
(which he hasnt)
hed abolish the bloomin thing's.

Give more able pupils copies of **Activity sheet 38 – Punctuation puzzles** to complete.

Can you punctuate this verse so that it makes sense?

Every lady in the land

every lady in the land

has twenty nails on each hand

five and twenty on hands and feet

this is true without deceit

Here's another poem without any punctuation and with no spaces between the words. If you write it out with proper spacing and punctuation it will help you to understand why we need to punctuate our writing.

whatspunctuation

whatspunctuationweallneed

itsothatwecanread

whatotherswritewithoutitwed

besoconfusedwewouldnotknow

ifweshouldstoporgo

onreadingwewouldlosetheflow

ofwhatthewritermeanttosay

yeswedallloseourway

sopunctuationsheretostay

Puns

A pun is the use of a word or phrase in order to create ambiguity.

Focus on puns

Explain what a pun is and that many jokes rely on a pun. This may be because of the sound of a word or because the word or phrase has a double meaning. An example of a pun based on a single word is this joke:

> What does a lion press most on his DVD player?
> Paws.

Point out that the pun in this joke is based on the homophones *paws* and *pause*.

Discuss the poems 'The woodworm', 'The kittens' and 'Crabs' and talk about how each one is based around a pun. Point out that the pun in each poem is based on a homonym (see p. 70)

The woodworm

The woodworm has few friends,
Because the main feature
Of the woodworm is that
It is a boring creature.

The kittens

All the kittens got excited,
When their Dad took first place
And won by six laps
In the milk-drinking race.

Crabs

There was a crime wave at the seaside.
There were thefts galore.
It was the crabs who were guilty.
They pinched everything they saw.

Make copies of **Activity sheet 39 – Question and answer jokes** and ask the pupils to complete the matching activity.

Activity sheet 39 – Question and answer jokes

Here are some question and answer jokes which are based on puns.
Match the answers to the questions.

Why can't a bicycle stand up?	It forgot to close its windows.
Why shouldn't you believe a person in bed?	Keep it waiting for hours.
Where do books sleep?	Because its mother was a wafer so long.
What do runners do when they forget something?	Because he is lying.
Why can't you tell a joke while ice-skating?	It gives a little whine.
Why was the computer cold?	He was trying to catch up on his sleep.
Why did the boy run around his bed?	It is too tired.
Why did the biscuit cry?	They try to jog their memory.
What happens if you sit on a grape?	Under their covers.
How do you make a monster stew?	The ice might crack up.

Extension activity

Explain that Knock Knock jokes are based on puns. Put some examples of Knock Knock jokes on the board, e.g. the ones included on the activity sheet. Discuss each one in turn and draw out how the joke is based on a pun. Ask the class to share any Knock Knock jokes they know and to find Knock Knock jokes in joke books. Invite them to make a class collection of Knock Knock jokes by copying them out, either to put on display or to put into a class book of Knock Knock jokes.

Hand out copies of **Activity sheet 40 – Knock Knock jokes** and invite pupils to write their own Knock Knock jokes to add to the class collection.

Activity sheet 40 – Knock Knock jokes

Knock Knock jokes always follow the same pattern.

The first two lines are the same:
Knock knock.
Who's there?

The third line is the person's name.
The fourth line is the person's name plus the question 'Who?'
The fifth line contains a pun based on the person's name.

Knock knock.
Who's there?
Carrie.
Carrie who?
Carrie on knocking until he opens the door.

Knock knock.
Who's there?
Percy.
Percy who?
Percy vere with these questions and you'll find out in the end.

Knock, knock.
Who's there?
Justin.
Justin who?
Justin case you hadn't realised, there's a gorilla on your roof.

Knock, knock.
Who's there?
Ivor.
Ivor who?
Ivor you open the door or I'll break it down.

Make up some Knock Knock jokes of your own, filling in the name in lines 3 and 4 and writing your own fifth line.

Knock knock.

Who's there?

_____

_____ who?

_____

Q is for...

Questions

A question is a form of sentence to which a response is required.

Focus on questions

Use the poem 'I am a question mark' and explain that a question always ends with the punctuation mark known as a question mark. When a question mark comes at the end of a sentence, it is followed by a capital letter.

I am a question mark

I am a question mark.
I sit on the keyboard
Waiting to be of service
In investigations and interrogations.
I help people with their enquiries.
If you're lost,
I can help you find the way.
If you're puzzled,
I can help you search for a solution.
If there's anything you need to know
Just ask
And I'll show
That an answer's expected.

Explain that many simple questions require a 'Yes' or 'No' answer. Other questions require a more open answer and begin with one of these question words: *who/whom which what when where why how*.

Questions game

The **Yes/No Game** is played in pairs. In this game, the person answering the questions is allowed to give only the answer 'yes' (or alternatively only the answer 'no') to every question asked. Pairs take it in turns to be the questioner and see how quickly they can get the other person to give an answer that is other than 'yes'. Time how long it takes before the person fails to answer 'yes'. The person who keeps on answering 'yes' for the longest time is the winner.

Language opportunities

When you are doing a history topic, you can do a hot seating activity in which one person takes on a role and answers questions put to him by other members of the class. For example, when they are learning about the Romans you can ask someone to play the part of a soldier who took part in building Hadrian's Wall. Take the opportunity to remind the class that they should ask questions to discover who, what, why, how, when and where the wall was built.

R is for...

Rhymes

Words which have the same final sound or sounds are said to make a rhyme.

Focus on rhymes

Explain what a rhyme is. Use **Activity sheet 41 – Rhymes** and ask the pupils to complete it individually or in pairs. The missing rhymes are: *class pass care wear state late matter chatter grin din day play dad bad report taught.*

Go through the rhymes in the poem and point out that words may end in the same sound, but the spelling of the sound may be different, as in the case of *care* and *wear*, both of which make the sound *–air.*

Introduce the idea of rhyme families – words that rhyme and have the same spelling of the sound.

Write the word *score* on the board and talk about its rhyme sound *–ore.* Ask the class to suggest words that rhyme with it, such as *more, roar, claw* and *door.* Collect their suggestions in columns, according to how the *–ore* sound is spelt.

–ore	–oar	–aw	–or	–oor	–our	other
score	roar	claw	nor	door	pour	dinosaur
more	oar	paw	meteor	floor	your	war
shore	soar	draw	corridor		four	drawer
before		saw	or			
explore		jaw				
galore		law				
ignore		raw				
snore		straw				
swore		thaw				
tore						
wore						

Invite the children to make up a rhyme or a tongue-twister using as many words with the −ore sound as possible.

You can end the focus on rhymes by explaining that there are some words that it is virtually impossible to find a rhyme for, unless you bend the rules. One of them is *month*.

> 'You can't', says Tom to lisping Bill,
> 'Find any rhyme for month.'
> 'A great mistake', was Bill's reply.
> 'I've found a rhyme at onth!'

Other words that have no rhymes are *oblige, orange, restaurant, silver, purple* and *penguin*.

Think of a Rhyme

This is a word game for any number of players. You start by choosing a word from this list of words: *bear cake cat chin clap crack day deer goat hill light nose rain roar snail snow spy sweet test tree weed.*

The first player says the chosen word, e.g. *goat*. The other players have to take it in turns to think of a word that rhymes with *goat*. When a person is stuck they say 'pass' and the round continues until no one can think of any more words that rhyme with *goat*.

Mime the Rhyme

This is a word game for two teams. One team chooses a word, such as *car*, and then gives the other team a clue telling them a word which rhymes with *car*. For example, they might say 'Our word rhymes with guitar.'

The members of the other team then try to guess the word you have chosen by thinking of words that rhyme with *guitar* and then miming them.

The first team has to identify the word being mimed. For example, the second team might mime *jar*. When the first team has identified *jar*, they must tell the second team whether the word is right. If it is wrong, the second team must mime another word, and continue miming words until they either find the right word or they give up.

Keep scores for the teams by adding a point every time they mime a word that isn't right. The team with the lowest number of points at the end of the game is the winner.

The rhyming words have been left out of this poem.
Can you fill them in?

Children's prayer

Let the teachers of our _____

Set us tests that we all _____.

Let them never ever _____

About what uniform we _____.

Let them always clearly _____

It's OK if your homework's _____.

Let them say it doesn't _____

When we want to talk and _____.

Let our teachers shrug and _____

When we make an awful _____.

Let them tell us every _____

There are no lessons. Go and _____.

Let them tell our mum and _____

That we are good and never _____.

Let them say in their _____

We are the best class they have _____.

Riddles

In a riddle you write about something without telling the reader what it is. The reader has to work out what it is from the clues you give.

Focus on riddles

Explain what a riddle is and that some riddles consist of a simple question, e.g. 'What holds water but is full of holes?' Answer: 'A sponge.'

Discuss how many Christmas crackers contain riddles that are simple questions. The answers are often based on a play on words or pun. You could ask them if they know the answers to the five Christmas cracker riddles (below), then invite them to share similar riddles that they already know.

Q. Why did the lobster blush? A. Because it saw the salad dressing.

Q. Why do history teachers like fruit cake? A. Because it is full of dates.

Q. Why are some snakes good at sums? A. Because they are adders.

Q. Why couldn't the witch's victim move? A. Because he was spellbound.

Q. Why was the vampire's bank account always in the red? A. Because it was in a blood bank.

Other riddles are in verse. Put a number of verse riddles on the board and divide the class into groups. See which group can be the first to answer all the riddles. Answers: 1 ball 2 pea 3 bottle 4 shoe 5 snow 6 a pair of gloves 7 greenhouse.

Verse riddles

1. I can spin. I can roll. I can fly through the air.
   I go where you hit me. Then I lie waiting there.
   I am usually round – sometimes big, sometimes small.
   I can make my way over or back from a wall.

2. I'm inside a whistle and inside speak.
   I'm found in a pod and a mountain's peak.

3. What has a neck, but not a head
   And sits on a bar or a shelf,
   Wearing a metal or plastic cap
   That it cannot remove itself.

4. What has eyes, but it cannot see
   And a tongue but it cannot talk
   Sounds as if it has a soul,
   Is a foot long and helps you to walk.

5. What falls more in winter
   Than falls in the fall?
   And covers the house
   In a white overall?
   What has a soft landing
   Wherever it falls?
   What is shaped into people
   And rolled into balls?

6. We each have four fingers and a thumb
   But of flesh and bone we have none.
   In the cold we can stop you from feeling numb.

7. I sound as if I'm the colour of grass
   And most of me is made of glass.
   Inside me the seeds you sew
   Are sure to keep warm and grow.

Encourage the children to find riddles in books and on the internet and to print them out to put on the classroom wall.

Make copies of **Activity sheet 42 – Write a riddle** and invite the children to write their own riddles. Stress that though the example rhymes, they need not make their riddles rhyme.

Extension activity

Give out copies of **Activity sheet 43 – Riddles** for more able pupils to solve.

The answers are: stomach, phantom, bookworm, graveyard, nightmare. You can then challenge them to write similar riddles.

Language opportunities

A good time to introduce work on riddles is in the run-up to Christmas. You can start with a discussion of Christmas cracker riddles (see above) as a lead into more detailed work on riddles.

How to write a riddle

Here's how John Foster planned and wrote a riddle about a squirrel

Choose subject →	Note the details →	Compare it to other things →	Draft the riddle
↓	↓	↓	↓
a grey squirrel	bushy tail hibernates grey fur digs up and eats nuts	tail like a fox scampers like a rabbit as grey as ash	rhyming or not rhyming? will try to rhyme

This is the riddle that John wrote:

> I scamper up the trunks of trees.
> I leap from branch to branch with ease.
> My fur is coloured like ash, it's grey.
> In winter I hide myself away.
> Like a rabbit, I scrape the ground,
> Then chew the buried nuts I've found.

Now write your own riddle:

Choose an animal or an object.

Write down some details about it.

Compare it to other things.

Draft your riddle.

Can you solve these riddles?

In the following riddles, you have to work out what the word is letter by letter.

Who am I (1)?

My first is in fish but not in chip.
My second in teeth but not in lip.
My third's in potato but not in plum.
My fourth's in mouth and also in thumb.
My fifth is in pear but not in cherry.
My sixth is in bacon but not in berry.
My last is in chocolate but not in crumble.
Sometimes when I'm empty you'll hear me rumble.

Who am I (2)?

My first is in spirit, but not in haunt.
My second is in haggard, but not in gaunt.
My third is in grave and also in dead.
My fourth is in fiend, but not in dread.
My fifth is in ghost, but not in scare.
My sixth is in torment, but not in nightmare.
My seventh is in demon, but not in fright.
I appear at the opera night after night.

In these riddles, the first and second lines each describe a word. The third line gives a clue as to how the words described in the first two lines fit together to make the word that is the answer.

1. My first is filled with pages of words.
    My second is found wriggling in the ground.
    My whole loves to read.

2. My first is serious and a last resting place.
    My second is three feet long.
    My third is full of the dead.

3. My first comes after day is done.
    My second will take you for a ride.
    My third will wake you and leave you shaking.

Similes

A simile is when you compare one thing to another in order to create an image in the reader's mind using *like* or *as* to make the comparison.

Focus on similes

Explain what a simile is. Using **Activity sheet 44 – Similes poems**, put the poem 'As slippery as...' on the board. Discuss how it consists of a list of similes, then invite the children to write a similar similes poem of their own.

Put the two comparison poems about a cat and a crocodile on the board and discuss their patterns, then ask the children to write their own poems about an animal, using a similar pattern.

Language opportunities

The work on similes can be linked to the activities on clichés, which ask the children to think of alternatives for clichéd similes.

Activity sheet 44 – Similes poems

The poem 'As slippery as…' consists of a list of similes. Choose an adjective and write your own poem which is a list of similes. For example, 'As strong as…', 'As soft as…', 'As brave as…' Be as original as you can and avoid using clichés.

As slippery as…

An icy puddle,
A bar of soap,
Soft ice cream
As it slides down your throat.

A water slide,
A squirming fish,
The end of a rainbow,
A whispered wish.

Comparison poems

These two poems have the same pattern. The first three lines consist of similes, the fourth line is a general comment about the animal which is the subject of the poem and the fifth line names the animal.

Eyes gleaming like green glass
Body tense as a spring
Claws like unsheathed daggers
Watching, waiting to pounce –
Cat.

Skin wrinkled like tree bark
Still as a log
Jaws gaping like a steel trap
Ready to snap shut –
Crocodile.

Write your own poem about an animal using the same pattern. Choose an animal or insect as the subject of the poem. For example: *dog rat lion cheetah spider wasp snake monkey gorilla fox.*

Work in groups and compile an A to Z of similes. Here's the start of one Encourage more able pupils to try to make it rhyme.

As agile as a monkey
As busy as a bee
As calm as a sleeping cat
As deep as the cold dark sea…

Slang

Slang is a particular type of language used in informal situations. There are many slang terms in widespread use, e.g. *gobsmacked* (amazed) and *gutted* (very disappointed).

There are quite a lot of slang terms for money and not having any money. This short verse contains some of them.

I wish I had plenty of dosh

I wish I had plenty of dosh.
I wish I had lots of bread.
I need wads of readies.
I need loads of lolly.
But I'm broke. I'm skint instead.

Focus on slang

Put a copy of 'I wish I had plenty of dosh' on the whiteboard. Explain what the term 'slang' means and ask the class if they can think of other slang terms connected with money, e.g. dough, broke, hard up.

Point out that slang words are more common in speech than in writing, because they are regarded as inappropriate in formal writing, such as schoolwork.

Make copies of **Activity Sheet 45 – A dictionary of slang**. Invite groups to prepare entries for a dictionary of slang. You could collect their entries together in a class dictionary of slang.

Make copies of **Activity Sheet 46 – Talk like a pirate** for each pupil. Explain that you are going to focus on pirate slang and that they are going to practise talking like a pirate. (Every year, 19 September is Talk Like a Pirate Day and you could plan to join in.)

Begin by focusing on pirate vocabulary. Talk about the words and phrases used in the poem and together with the class build up a list on the whiteboard. Other words and phrases you could add include 'avast!', 'aye aye!' and 'Davy Jones's locker'.

Go through the other points one by one. Remind them of what the tense of a verb is, when discussing speaking in the present tense only and point out the use of the apostrophe when a letter is omitted in a word.

Similarly, remind the pupils what an adjective is when discussing how pirates exaggerate things by using two adjectives instead of one.

When you have fully explained how to talk like a pirate, ask the children in groups to practise acting out the scenes. At the end of the session, invite the groups to take turns performing their scenes to the rest of the class.

Language opportunities

When studying the Second World War, you could introduce the fact that RAF pilots developed their own slang. For example, 'prang' was a crash and 'gen' was information. You could put the following sentences up on the board and ask the class if they can work out what the slang terms mean:

> 'It was a dicey op. We took a lot of flak and almost bought it. We nearly had to ditch our kite in the drink. But we made it to the drome.'

Work on slang can be linked to work on formal and informal language, and can arise, for example, when working on playscripts.

Some slang words are included in a dictionary. Here is an entry for the word 'bloke':

>   **bloke** (noun: an informal word) A bloke is a man

The entry tells you what type of word it is as well as its meaning.

Sometimes a word has two meanings. Here is the entry for the word 'clobber' which has two meanings:

>   **clobber** (an informal word)
>   1. (noun) You can call someone's belongings their clobber
>   2. (verb) If you clobber someone, you hit them

Write some entries for a dictionary of slang.

Start by making a list of slang words, e.g. *stroppy nut naff slob grub bonkers kid yob wannabee*

Choose some words from your list or from the list in the box.

Write some entries for your slang dictionary. If you are stuck for a definition of the word, look it up to see if it is in the dictionary and, if so, how it is defined.

Collect your entries in a class dictionary of slang.

Activity sheet 46 – Talk like a pirate

Shiver me timbers! Yo-ho-ho!

Shiver me timbers! Yo-ho-ho!
Arrr, arrr, arrr, me hearty!
There's a tot of grog, you scurvy dog,
If you sail with our pirate party.

How to talk like a pirate

1. Use pirate vocabulary. Make a list of words and phrases that pirates use, with their meanings, e.g. 'Ahoy!' means 'Hullo, there!'
2. Use insults like 'You scurvy dog!', 'You be nothin' but a bilge rat!', 'You ol' landlubber!'
3. Speak only in the present tense and say *I be, you be, he be, we be* and *they be*, instead of *I am, you are, he is, we are* and *they are*.
4. Drop your Hs at the beginning of words, e.g. 'I'd 'ang 'im from the yardarm.'
5. Drop the G from words ending in *–ing* so that you say *fightin'* instead of *fighting* and *scrubbin'* instead of *scrubbing*.
6. Leave out the V when you say words such as *never, ever* and *over*, so that you say *ne'er, e'er* and *o'er*.
7. Exaggerate what you have to say by always using two adjectives where one would do. For example, describe someone as 'a slimy rotten bilge rat' rather than just 'a slimy bilge rat' or as 'a lazy idle layabout' instead of just 'a lazy layabout'.
8. Start a lot of what you say with 'Arrr' and always say *me* for *my* and *thar* for *there*.

Act like a pirate

1. Act out a scene in which a group of pirates are looking at a treasure map and arguing about the exact spot where they have buried their treasure. They could even be arguing about whether they are looking at the right island.
2. Act out a scene in which a group of pirates are sitting celebrating the successful capture of a treasure ship and talking about what they plan to do with the prisoners they've taken and where they plan to hide the booty they've stored in the hold.
3. Act out a scene in which a young boy, who wants to become a pirate, tries to persuade a pirate captain and his mate to let him join their crew.

Spelling

Spelling a word means writing its letters in the correct order.

Focus on spelling

Put the poem 'It's a mystery' up on the board. Explain that English words are often difficult to spell because they are not spelt as they sound. The reason for this is the way the language developed, borrowing words from so many other languages.

Discuss the different spellings of sounds that are mentioned in the poem and point out that *oar* is also spelt differently from *draw*, *door*, *pour* and *ignore*.

It's a mystery

English spelling is a real mystery.
Why isn't mystery spelt like history?
If words make the same sound, as many do,
Surely they should be spelt the same too.

If it is huff and puff, and gruff and stuff,
Why isn't tough tuff and enough enuff?
And why when draw makes the same sound as door,
Aren't they spelt like pour or ignore?

Why English spelling is a mystery
Is due to the language's history.

Focus on spelling rules

Explain that there are a number of spelling rules that are helpful. But there are always a number of exceptions.

i before e except after c

Read the poem 'i before e', explain the rule and write 'i before e except after c' on the board. Exceptions to the rule include weir and weird.

i before e

As a rule it's *i* before *e*
Except when they come after *c*.
In belief and in grief there's no *c*
So they are spelled *i* before *e*.
In receive there's a *c* and that's why
When we write it we put *e* before *i*.

Dropping the final e

When adding a suffix like *–ed* or *–ing*
To a verb that ends with an *e*
Because the suffix starts with a vowel
We drop the *e*, you see.

Write the poem on the board and give an example:

hope + *–ed* = hoped, hope + *–ing* = hoping

Then ask the children to give further examples and list some on the board.

Explain that the rule is: if you add a suffix beginning with a vowel to a word ending in *–e*, then you drop the final *e*.

So excite + ed = excited, excite + ing = exciting, but excite + ment = excitement; care + ed = cared care + ing = caring but care + less = careless

Give the class a quick quiz. Ask them what happens to the final 'e' when you join the suffixes in brackets to these particular words:

1. give (ing)
2. hope (less)
3. amaze (ment)
4. stare (ed)
5. lone (ly)
6. whistle (ing)
7. daze (ed)
8. spite (ful)
9. achieve (ment)
10. exclusive (ly)

Dropping the final l

Read the poem and make sure that the children understand that the rule is when we add *–full* to the end of a word we drop the final *l*. List examples on the board.

Point out that when the suffix *–ly* is added to a word ending in *l*, then there will be a double *l*. Give some examples: *hopefully, eventually, carefully.*

> I'm playful and joyful and hopeful
> That you'll be able to tell
> That when we add *–full* to a word
> We drop the final *l*.

Words ending in y

Changing the y to an i

Write examples to show how words which end with a consonant followed by a *y* change the y to an i when adding a suffix. Before you tell the pupils the rule, see if they can work it out for themselves.

party + es = parties;	spy + es = spies
study + ed = studied;	hurry + ed = hurried
beauty + ful = beautiful;	mercy + ful = merciful
mystery + ous = mysterious;	glory + ous = glorious
happy + ness = happiness;	lonely + ness = loneliness

When the y does not change

Once they have understood the rule, explain that the rule does not apply when you add the suffix *–ing*. The *y* does not change to an *i*.

Give some examples: hurry + ing = hurrying; study + ing = studying.

Explain that words which end in a vowel followed by a *y* do not drop the *y* when adding *–s*, *–ed* and *–ing*.

Give some examples: *plays played playing obeys obeyed obeying boys toys.*

Doubling the final consonant

Explain that when you add *–ed* or *–ing* to some words, you double the consonant.

Rule 1: If the word is a one-syllable word ending with the pattern consonant – vowel – consonant, then you double the consonant.

Examples: rip + *–ed* = ripped; scrub + *–ed* = scrubbed

sit + *–ing* = sitting; star + *–ing* = starring

However, this rule does not apply
If a word ends in *w, x* or *y*.
Snow becomes snowed,
Say becomes saying,
While box is boxing,
And play is playing.

Rule 2: If the word is a two–syllable word ending with the pattern consonant – vowel – consonant and the stress is on the second syllable, then you double the consonant.

> Examples: oc**cur** + *–ed* = occurred; per**mit** + *–ed* = permitted
> be**gin** + *–ing* = beginning; pre**fer** + *–ing* = preferring

But if the stress is on the first syllable you do not double the consonant.

> **hap**pen + *–ed* = happened; **o**pen + *–ed* = opened
> **fright**en + *–ing* = frightening; **en**ter + *–ing* = entering

Hard c and soft c

Explain that the letter *c* can make a different sound in different words.

> It makes a hard *k* sound when it comes before the vowels *a, o* and *u*.
> Examples are *card, cold* and *custard*.

> It makes a soft *s* sound when it comes before the vowels *e, i* and *y*.
> Examples are centre, circle and cymbal.

Put the class into groups and give each group a large sheet of paper. Ask one of them to draw six columns on the paper and to label the columns *a o u i e y*. Then ask them to think of words beginning with *c* and to list those with a hard *c* sound in the columns *a, o* and *u* and those with a soft *c* sound in the columns *i, e* and *y*. To make sure they understand, draw the six columns on the board and demonstrate what they have to do by putting a word in each column. Encourage them to use dictionaries to help them.

Hard c		
a	o	u
card	cold	custard

Soft c		
e	i	y
century	city	cycle

Extension activity

Play the game **Hard c versus Soft c**.

Hard c versus Soft c

This is a game for two pairs. Each pair is given a piece of paper. The first pair must write a sentence in which they use three words with a hard *c* in them, e.g. 'The cat was covered in custard.' The other pair have to write a sentence in which there are three words with a soft *c* in them, e.g. 'I cycled to the city centre.' The players then swap their pieces of paper. The first pair must write a sentence using three soft *c* words, but they cannot use the ones already used. The second pair must write a sentence using three different hard *c* words. The game continues until one pair is unable to think of three new words to make a sentence.

Hard g and Soft g

Explain that the letter *g* can make a different sound in different words.

It makes a hard *g* sound when it comes before the vowels *a, o* and *u*. Examples are *gate, go,* and *gum*.

It makes a soft *g* sound like a *j* when it comes before the vowels *e, i* and *y*. Examples are *geography, ginger* and *gym*.
But there are exceptions such as *gift, girl* and *giggle*.

Draw three columns on the board under the heading 'Hard g', labelled a, o and u, and three columns under the heading 'Soft g' labelled e, i and y. Ask the class for words beginning with *g* to list in each column. Use a black pen and have a red pen handy, so that you can highlight exceptions like *girl* and *giggle*.

Focus on silent letters

Use **Activity sheet 47 – Silent letters**. Talk about each poem in turn.
Explain that the silent *b* occurs in words which have an *m* before the *b*. Examples of other words which end with a silent *b* are *bomb, comb, lamb, limb* and *succumb*.

Some words, which sound as though they should start with an *n*, start with a silent *g* or a silent *k*. Other words not included in the poem which start with a silent *k* are: *knack, knave, knell, knife, knob, knoll* and *knot*.

Some words which sound as though they should start with an *r* start with a silent *w*.

Other words, not included in the poem, which start *wr—* include *wrack, wrangle, wreath, wren, wrest, wring, wrought* and *wry*.

We're the silent 'b's

We're the silent 'b's.
We can make you numb.
We can stop your chatter
By making you dumb.

We can help clean up
By picking up crumbs.
We can show we approve
By sticking up thumbs.

The silent 'g's

The silent 'g's are coming,
They may be nearing you.
The gnarled gnome, the gnat
And the gnashing, gnawing gnu.

I am a silent k

I am a silent k.
Without me
Someone might nick your knickers
Or nap in your knapsack.
You need me to be able to knead
To knock or to kneel.
I can help you
To knuckle down to knitting.
I have the knack.
Sir K, that's me –
A knowledgeable knight.

The silent 'w's

Here come the silent 'w's,
Wriggling and writhing along
Wreaking havoc with your spelling –
If you write rong, that's wrong!

As you wrestle with wrinkle and wreck,
With wrapper, wrench, wretched and wrist,
Watch out for the silent ws,
They're wrathful if ever they're missed.

Draw four columns labelled "Silent 'b's", "Silent 'g's", "Silent 'k's" and "Silent 'w's", and make lists of words which end with a silent *b*, or start with a silent *g*, a silent *k* or a silent *w*. Use a dictionary to help you with your lists.

© 2012, *Learning about Language: Activities for the Primary Classroom*, John Foster, Routledge

Letter patterns –gh and –ght

Explain that the letter pattern *–gh* in some words makes the sound *f* and in other words is silent. Put a copy of the poem 'Sound advice' on the board and then invite the children to play **Pass It On**.

Sound advice

Put g and h together
In cough and rough and tough
And they make the sound of 'f'-
In trough and in enough.

But g and h together
In the pattern ght,
In fight and right, caught, taught and nought,
Is then silent, you see.

In several other words
gh is silent too,
In dough and though, bough and plough
In thorough and in through.

Pass It On

The aim is to make up a story with *–gh* and *–ght* words in it. The first person starts the story by writing a sentence on a piece of paper with a word that has either *–gh* or *–ght* in it. He then passes the paper to another person, who has to add another sentence with a *–gh* or *–ght* word on it, and so on. If anyone is unable to think of a word, she say 'pass', and passes the paper on.

At the end of the game, someone can type up a copy of the story with all the *–gh* and *–ght* words highlighted to put on display.

Letter pattern –ation

Explain that there are lots of words in English that end with the letter pattern *–ation* (pronounced 'ayshun'). Make a collection of them on the board, then write them on cards and make a chain of *–ation* words to hang from the ceiling. Here is a list of twenty common *–ation* words that you can include on your word chain: *abbreviation cancellation celebration conversation creation destination education examination generation illustration multiplication nation operation punctuation radiation registration relation relegation station vacation.*

Spoonerisms

A spoonerism is an accidental slip of the tongue so that you swap the first letters or sometimes the syllables of words. As a result you create a ludicrous or nonsensical phrase or statement.

Focus on spoonerisms

Explain what a spoonerism is and that they are named after the Reverend William Spooner (1844–1930), the Warden of New College, Oxford, who had the habit of mixing up words in this way. Among the sayings attributed to the Reverend Spooner are:

Please sew me to my sheet.
You have tasted the whole worm.
Cyclists need well-boiled icicles.

Put a copy of **Activity Sheet 48 – Spoonerisms** on the whiteboard. Explain that each sentence contains a spoonerism and ask them to write down what the person actually meant to say. Point out that that each short verse contains a number of spoonerisms and ask the pupils in pairs to work out what the poets actually meant to write.

Remind them what a proverb is (p. 115). Put these proverbs on the board and discuss what the actual proverbs are.

Let sleeping logs die.
Out of the prying fan into the fire.
You can't tell a book by cooking at its lover.

Extension activity

Ask any linguistically gifted children in the class if they can make up some spoonerisms. Then invite them to share their spoonerisms with the class.

Activity sheet 48 – Spoonerisms

A spoonerism is a slip of the tongue, i.e. a tip of the slung. Here are some spoonerisms. Write down what the person meant to say.

I saw a flutterby.

I hurt my bunny phone.

I was shaking a tower.

He told a lack of pies.

It was roaring with pain.

I hanged my bed on the ceiling.

Here are some powers I flicked.

I was faking a tree-kick.

It lost a cot of money.

I fit a liar to burn the rubbish.

Here are some short verses each containing spoonerisms. Can you work out what the poets meant to write?

I was waking the dog for a talk

I was waking the dog for a talk
In the dark one summer's pay.
The dog trotted a cat by a spree.
The bog darked and the rat can away.

On a dot summer's hay

On a dot summer's hay
I was saying by the plea,
When my Dad crowned a fab
Which knit him on the bee!

I bit a hall

I bit a hall
It skew up in the fly
And handed on the lead
Of a rat cunning by.

Syllables

A syllable is a unit of sound which forms a word or part of a word.

Focus on syllables

Explain what a syllable is and give examples: *head* has one syllable, *headland* has two syllables and *headteacher* has three syllables.

Point out that you can find out how many syllables a word has by clapping out the beats. Try clapping out these words: gargantuan (4), geography (4), mystery (3), emergency (4). Link the words you choose either to your current topic or to long words that you have noticed the pupils misspelling, such as *dis-ap-point*.

Breaking down a word into syllables can be particularly useful when trying to spell a long word, such as *investigation*, which has five syllables: *–in –vest –ig –a –tion*.

Language opportunities

Take the opportunity to remind them what syllables are when looking at forms of poetry, which are patterned according to the number of syllables in each line, such as haiku, cinquains and diamond poems.

Use **Activity sheet 49 – Haiku**. Discuss what a haiku is and the example given. Then draft a class haiku which provides a snapshot of a scene, e.g. at a fair, a circus or a zoo, before asking the children to write their own haikus.

Also, put a copy of the two poems from **Activity sheet 50 – Cinquains** on the board. Explain what a cinquain is and discuss the two examples before inviting the children to draft their own.

Using **Activity sheet 51 – Diamond poems**, discuss how a diamond poem is patterned, then draft a class diamond poem on the board, before inviting individuals to draft a diamond poem.

You can end the focus on syllables with these interesting word facts:

The word *screeched* is the longest single-syllable word in the English language.

The word *are*, which has only one syllable, can be made into a three-syllable word by adding only one letter —*a*— making the word *area*. You can also make *rode* into *rodeo* by adding the letter *o* and, similarly, make *came* into *cameo* by adding an *o*.

The word *monosyllable* has five syllables in it.

A haiku is a Japanese form of poem. It is made up of three lines and seventeen syllables. The first line has five syllables, the second has seven, and the third has five.

A haiku is like a snapshot poem. A good haiku creates a clear picture, based on close observation. Here are three examples:

Bright as butterflies
With folded wings, the windsurfs
Skim across the bay.

Locked in its hutch,
The pet rabbit does not know
The freedom of fields.

Pale lemon primroses
Whispering promises of summer
On a dull March day.

Draft a haiku of your own in which you create a picture by making a comparison. Either choose a subject of your own or write about one of the following: a pet animal or a zoo animal, a wild bird, a type of flower or tree.

....

....

....

Activity sheet 50 – Cinquains

A cinquain consists of five lines containing twenty-two syllables in the pattern 2-4-6-8-2. Often a cinquain describes a particular sound or sight. Notice how in these two examples each poet uses a comparison to describe the particular sound and sight.

November night, by Adelaide Crapsey

Listen...
With faint dry sound
Like steps of passing ghosts,
The leaves, frost-crisped, break from the trees
And fall.

Storm at sea, by John Foster

Boats ride
The switchback waves.
Like rollercoaster cars,
They climb and dip towards harbour's
Haven.

Write a cinquain that describes a particular sound or sight. Try to use a comparison in the way that Adelaide Crapsey and John Foster do.

....

....

....

....

....

Activity sheet 51 – Diamond poems

In a diamond poem, the words together form the shape of a diamond. To make the shape, they have a specific syllable pattern: 1-2-3-4-5-4-3-2-1. Diamond poems can be written on any subject. Here are two examples:

Snow –
Soft flakes
Dust the street,
Painting pavements
A   brilliant   white.
In the lamp's light,
Glittering
Crystals
Gleam.

Wind
Whistling
Down chimneys
Whipping windows
Ripping tiles off roofs
Snapping at trees –
A howling
Wild wolf
Wind.

Draft a diamond poem of your own. Either choose a subject that appeals to you or choose one from this list: sun, moon, stars, rain, trees, deer, cows, hens, sheep, cat, dog, fire, clocks, storm, sea.

Synonyms

A synonym is a word which means the same or nearly the same as another word. For example: start/begin, end/finish, journey/trip.

Focus on synonyms

Explain what a synonym is and how synonyms can be found in a thesaurus – a reference book in which words are grouped according to their meanings. Talk about how a thesaurus can help writers when searching for a word which means precisely what they want to say and to avoid words that have lost their effectiveness through over-use.

Write the entries from a thesaurus for *sad* and *happy* on the board. Talk about the alternatives which are listed. Ask the pupils which they think are the two most powerful alternatives for *sad* and which are the two most powerful alternatives to *happy*.

> **sad** unhappy miserable glum gloomy low depressed dejected downcast
> despondent
> **happy** cheerful joyful delighted overjoyed thrilled pleased gleeful ecstatic
> elated

Invite the pupils in groups to write some thesaurus entries.

Make Your Own Thesaurus

Write a number of thesaurus entries. Work in groups and draw up your entries without consulting a thesaurus. Then check your entries against those in a thesaurus and add any words that you find in it that are not on your list.

Either choose your own words or write entries for words from this list: *big small foul angry loud fierce lonely slow fast ugly.*

Supply a Synonym

Play **Supply a Synonym**, a word game for groups of five or more. The game begins with everyone sitting in a circle. The youngest in the group chooses a word that is widely used, e.g. *talk*. The person sitting to the left then has to supply a synonym, e.g. *say, speak, utter, chatter*. The next player on the left then has to supply another synonym. The round continues until someone is stuck and unable to provide another synonym, and is eliminated. The person who is eliminated chooses another word for the next round. The rounds continue until only one person is left as the winner.

Extension activity – Antonyms

Explain that an antonym is the opposite of a synonym. It is a word which means the opposite of another word.

Put 'Dr Scotby's advice on how to behave' on the board and talk about how each line of this poem contains a word or expression followed by an antonym.

Dr Scotby's advice on how to behave

Be careful, don't be reckless.
Be polite, do not be rude.
Be brave, not cowardly.
Show good taste and don't be crude.

Be courteous, not ill-mannered.
Neither submit, nor defy.
Be punctual, not late.
Tell the truth and do not lie.

Invite the class to have fun with antonyms. Put the following passage on the board and ask them to rewrite it, replacing each of the underlined words with an antonym of that word, e.g. substituting *cowardly* for *brave*.

'The <u>brave</u> knight took a <u>deep</u> breath and stepped <u>cautiously</u> forward, his <u>sharp</u> sword at the ready. The <u>fierce</u> dragon lunged towards him, <u>thick</u> smoke pouring from its <u>huge</u> nostrils, its <u>bright</u> eyes gleaming. It opened its <u>vicious</u> jaws and gave a <u>loud</u> roar.'

Txtspk

txtspk (textspeak), also known as SMS language, is a form of language used to communicate on mobile phones when using the Short Message Service (SMS).

Focus on txtspk

Explain what is meant by SMS language. Point out that the use of textspeak was developed in order to keep messages short. So lots of abbreviations are used and punctuation is largely ignored. Only full stops and exclamation marks are widely used and there's usually no capital letter after a full stop.

Put 'A series of messages' on the board. Explain that it is an exchange of messages between two young girls. Ask the children what the messages said and write up how they would have been written if the girls had used Standard English.

Point out the different methods that are used in the messages to shorten words. Discuss the following points:

1. Single letters are used to replace words: *b* for *be*, *u* for *you* and *y* for **why**. Other examples are *c* for *see* and *r* for *are*.

2. Numbers are used for individual words, e.g. *2* for *to* and *4* for *for*, and are also used for parts of words which sound like the number, e.g. *w8* for *wait*, *l8* for *late* and *4get* for *forget*. Other examples are *of10* and *gr8*.

3. Words are shortened by leaving out the vowels. The words become just a string of consonants, but you can still recognise them, e.g. *bttr* for *better*, *agn* for *again*. Another example is *wkd* for *wicked*.

4. Slang words and spellings are used instead of conventional ones, e.g. *cos* for *because*, *skool* for *school* and *woz* for *was*. Other examples are *gratz* for *congratulations* and *nite* for *night*.

5. Words are spelt as they are pronounced, e.g. *wur* for *were*, *no* for *know*, *ud* for *you'd* and *ule* for *you'll*. Other examples are *ova* for *over* and *wiv* for *with*.

A series of messages

Jenny: y wur u l8 4 skool 2day
Sam: i hd 2 w8 4 k8
Jenny: y woz k8 l8
Sam: cos hr mum 4got to wke hr
Jenny: ud bttr not b l8 agn or ule b 4 it
Sam: i no

Explain that another way of shortening phrases or words is to abbreviate them by using only the first letter of the words. For example, *lol* means *laugh out loud*, *gg* means *good game*.

Give out **Activity sheet 52 – Txtspk** for the children to complete.

The children can compare Standard English messages and text messages by doing the exercises on **Activity sheet 53 – Messaging.**

Discuss how 'and' in the poem is written as an ampersand. Explain that the ampersand is a shorthand way of writing 'and'. Its most common use now is in textspeak, but you will also see it in the names of businesses, e.g. Jones & Sons.

Explain that the word 'ampersand' is derived from a phrase 'and per se and', which schoolchildren used to chant as a way of remembering that the symbol '&' means 'and'. The Latin words 'per se' mean 'by itself'. So the phrase the children chanted means '& by itself = and'.

Activity sheet 52 –Txtspk

What do the following letters stand for?

bbl

brb

gtg

idk

kk

lol

plz

rofl

thx

wb

Add some other examples of txtspk.

Imagine the messages that these people sent. First write them out in full, then write them as they would be sent as text messages.

1. What the Ugly Sisters sent to each other when the shoe was found to fit Cinderella.
2. What St George sent to the dragon before their contest.
3. What Little Bo Peep sent to say that her sheep were lost.
4. What Hercules sent after successfully completing one of his labours.
5. What Sleeping Beauty sent when she woke up.
6. What Odysseus sent after escaping from the Cyclops's cave.
7. What Jack sent after killing the giant.
8. What one of the King's men sent, to report that they couldn't put Humpty Dumpty together again.
9. What Aladdin sent after releasing the genie from the magic lamp.
10. What one of the children sent to Peter Pan after they were captured by pirates.

The use of numbers and single letters to represent a word or part of a word was thought of long before texting began. Study the poem (below). Work out what the poem says and write out a full version of it, which does not include any abbreviations.

To a sick friend

I'm in a 10der mood 2day,
    & feel poetic, 2;
4 fun I'll just – off a line
    & send it off 2 U.
I'm sorry you've been 6 o long;
    Don't B disconsol8;
But bear your ills with 42de,
    & they won't seem so gr8.
                            Anon.

Extension activity

Ask groups if they can solve this puzzle. The answer is: Too wise you are, Too wise you be. I see you are Too wise for me.

YY U R
YY U B
I C U R
YY 4 me.

Language opportunities

The Focus on Txtspk can be introduced alongside activities, which are aimed at developing the pupils' notemaking skills, for example, when they are studying a historical topic such as the Romans, the Vikings or Victorian England. SMS language is now a feature of the English language and can be useful when notemaking as it takes less time to write than standard English. It needs to be stressed, however, that while it is acceptable in note writing it is not acceptable in other types of writing.

Show pupils examples of how abbreviations similar to those used when texting can be used when taking notes. The Vikings can become *Viks*. Anglo-Saxons can become *A-S*. King can be *K* and Queen can be *Q*. Names can be shortened to initials – *JC* for Julius Caesar, *KH* for King Harold, *B* of Hastings for the Battle of Hastings. Place names can be abbreviated, e.g. *Eng.* for England, *Fr.* for France, *Eur.* for Europe and *Emp.* for Empire.

Encourage them to use common abbreviations, used in textspeak, such as bk for book, ch for church, gd for good, no for number, nr for near, r for river, rd for road and w for with. They can also use symbols such as = for equals and + or an ampersand for and.

Tongue-twisters

A tongue-twister is a rhyme or a sequence of words that is difficult to say because it uses similar or repeated sounds.

Focus on tongue-twisters

Explain what a tongue-twister is. Put these examples of tongue-twisters on the board. Allow them a few minutes to practise saying them, then hold a competition to see who can say them fastest.

> She sells sea shells on the sea shore.
> The shells that she sells are sea shells for sure.
> So, if she sells sea shells on the sea shore,
> That the sea shells are sea shore shells you can be sure.

> There's no need to light a night light
> On a light night like tonight;
> For a night light's just a slight light
> On a light night like tonight.

> I see icy seas.
> Icy seas I see.
> I freeze in icy seas.
> Icy seas freeze me.

Point out that the reason why many tongue-twisters are hard to say is because they contain a lot of alliteration – the use of several words together that all begin with the same letter or sound. Give some examples:

> Round and round the rugged rocks the ragged rascal ran.
> Gilly juggled jars of jelly.

Rhona rowed down the river, while Rhoda rode down the road, beside the river down which Rhona rowed.

Encourage the children to have a go at writing some tongue-twisters of their own. Tell them to begin by choosing a letter or two letters that make the same sound, such as *b*, *bl* or *br*. They should brainstorm all the words that they can think of beginning with the chosen letter or letters. They can then draft a tongue-twister, which consists of a single sentence, e.g.

Bruno, the brawny bear from Brighton, had a breakfast of broccoli and brown bread.

Alternatively, they can follow the pattern of this counting rhyme:

Five flustered fireflies flickering.
Four furry foxes foraging.
Three free fleas fleeing.
Two floppy fish floundering.
One flapping fly fluttering.

US English

US English or American English differs in a number of ways from British English. For example, there are differences in pronunciation, vocabulary, spelling and grammar.

Focus on American English

Explain that there are a number of differences between American English and British English. One of the differences is in vocabulary. Put the poem 'Understanding Uncle Sam' on the board and explain that Uncle Sam is the nickname given to the whole population who are citizens of the United States.

The nickname first appeared early in the nineteenth century, partly because army supplies had the initials US on them. Whether there was a real person called Uncle Sam, who was connected with army supplies, is not known.

Discuss the American terms that are included in the poem and write down what they mean (candy – sweets, sidewalk – pavement, fall –autumn, trunk – boot, hood – bonnet, cookie – biscuit, auto – car, gasoline – petrol, prom – formal dance held at a school or college).

Give out copies of **Activity sheet 54 – American English** for pairs or groups to complete. Encourage them to use dictionaries on the computer to find out the meanings of words that are new to them.

Explain that some spellings are different in American English. Put the table of common words on the board (see p. 181) and talk about the differences between the British and the American spellings.

British spelling	American spelling
colour	color
honour	honor
labour	labor
centre	center
fibre	fiber
litre	liter
defence	defense
offence	offense
cheque	check
pyjamas	pajamas
plough	plow
moustache	mustache

Extension activity

Explain that as well as differences in vocabulary and spelling there are small differences in grammar, and give some examples of expressions which are therefore different:

British expression	American expression
twenty to five	twenty of five
five past seven	five after seven
Monday to Friday inclusive	Monday through Friday

In American English, expressions are also often shortened, for example, by leaving out the word 'and' in expressions such as: I'll go see if it's ready; I'll try find out, which in British English would be: I'll go *and* see if it's ready and I'll try *and* find out.

Also, whereas British people say, I'm going out on Monday evening, Americans say, I'm going out Monday evening.

Understanding Uncle Sam

Can you skip down the sidewalk to the candy store?
Can you fall in the fall on the forest floor?
Can you open the trunk or the hood of a car?
Can you pick out a cookie from a cookie jar?

Can you fill up an auto with gasoline?
Can you make a date with the new prom queen?
If you can say 'You're welcome' and 'Howdy, ma'am'
You're on your way to understanding Uncle Sam.

Make a list of the American words used in this poem and their meanings.

Here is a list of other American words. Write their meanings in the space provided.

1. apartment	
2. cab	
3. diaper	
4. faucet	
5. line	
6. pacifier	
7. period	
8. recess	
9. stroller	
10. truck	
11. vacation	
12. yard	

V is for...

Vowels

In the alphabet, there are five letters which are vowels – a, e, i, o and u. Every syllable in a word contains a vowel.

Focus on vowels

Remind the class what a vowel is. To help them to understand how important vowels are in words, write the following sentences on the board leaving out all the vowels:

> Tk t yr bks. Trn t pg ght. Lk t th pctr. Wht d y s th ppl dng tsd th plc sttn?

Ask them in groups if they can work out what it means. Then write the words on the board with all the vowels in them.

> Take out your books. Turn to page eight. Look at the picture. What do you see the people doing outside the police station?

Discuss how some words are easier to understand without the vowels than others.

Then ask the pupils to look around the classroom and to pick out ten things that they can see, then to write down the words for them without any vowels in. Give them an example: dr for door.

Talk about how vowels are omitted from words when texting and build up a list of SMS words in which the vowels are left out.

Extension activity

Give groups of more able pupils **Activity Sheet 55 – Univocalics** to complete.

A univocalic is a piece of writing, for example a poem, which uses only words containing a single one of the five vowels.

Anna's all-star band

Anna has a band –
Anna's band raps raps –
Madcap ragbag claptrap raps.

Sharks snap jaws
Jackals jam jazz
Crabs clap claws –
Razzmatazz.

Llamas chant psalms
Swans twang saws
Carps clasp harps
And cats tap paws.

Ants bang pans
Rats rat-a-tat
A calf cancans
And yaks yak-yak.

Anna has a band –
Anna's band raps raps –
Madcap ragbag claptrap raps.

Univocalic challenge

Choose a vowel and make a list of words that contain only that vowel. Then see who can draft the longest sentence consisting of words that contain only that vowel.

Did you know?

- The longest word with a single vowel appearing only once is *strength.*
- *Defencelessness* is a fifteen-letter word in which the same vowel appears five times.
- The word *asthma* begins and ends with the same vowel and has no other vowel in between.
- *Abstemious, arsenious* and *facetious* are three of the few words that contain the five vowels in their alphabetical order.

Words

Focus on word formation – prefixes

Explain that many words in English have been formed by fixing a group of letters to an existing word in order to produce a new word with a different meaning. A group of letters added before a word is called a prefix.

Give out copies of **Activity sheet 56 – Prefixes** for the pupils to complete. Discuss other prefixes which are not on the list e.g. *bi–* (two), *fore–* (in front of), *fore–* (before), *mini–* (small), *re–* (again), *tri–* (three).

Discuss negative prefixes. The most common negative prefixes are *un–*, *dis–*, *il–*, *im–* and *ir–*. Draw three columns on the board with the headings 'Prefix', 'Example' and 'Meaning'. Write the negative prefixes in the first column, then ask the class to suggest examples. Point out words that are commonly misspelt such as *disappointment*, *disappear* and *unnecessary* and explain that remembering how they are formed can help you to remember how to spell these words. Your table might look like this:

Prefix	Example	Meaning
dis-	disobey	to refuse to follow orders
	disappointment	a feeling of being let down
	disappear	to vanish
il-	illegal	not legal
	illiterate	not able to read and write
in-	inexpensive	not costing a lot
	incredible	not believable
ir-	irrelevant	not relevant
	irreplaceable	not able to be replaced
mis-	misunderstand	not understand
	mistrust	not trust
un-	unhealthy	not healthy
	unnecessary	not necessary

Explain that the rule about spelling words with prefixes is:

You do not change the spelling of a word when adding a prefix to it.

This rule applies even when you add a prefix ending in *s* to a word starting with *s*.

dis + satisfy = dissatisfy
mis + spell = misspell

All and *well* are exceptions.
When you add *all* or *well* to a word, you drop one *l*.

all + together = altogether; well + come = welcome

Invite the pupils to do the **Negatives Challenge**.

The Negatives Challenge

This is a game for two or more pairs. The aim is to draw up a list of words that can be made to have a negative or opposite meaning by adding a prefix, such as *un–*. Set a time limit, e.g. five minutes, and the winners are the pair who list the most words.

Have a dictionary to hand in order to check any disputed words, but do not cheat by referring to it during the game.

You can play several rounds using different prefixes: *un–*, *dis–*, *il–*, *im–* ,*in–* and *ir–*.

A word of advice: you need to be careful with words beginning with *im–*, *in–* and *ir–* as they can also mean 'into' in words such as *imprison, intimidate* and *irradiate*.

Activity sheet 56 – Prefixes

Prefix	Meaning	Examples
anti-	against	antifreeze
auto-	self	autograph
ex-	out of	extract
inter-	between	international
mal-	bad	maltreat
multi-	many	multi-storey
over-	over	overthrow
post-	after	postscript
pre-	before	predict
semi-	half	semi-final
sub-	under	submarine
super-	more than	superstore
trans-	across	transform
under-	under	underground

The list contains many of the most common English prefixes.
Complete the table by adding further examples of words which are
made by adding these prefixes. Use a dictionary to help you.

Focus on word formation – suffixes

Explain that many words in English are words that have been formed by fixing a group of letters to an existing word in order to produce a new word with a different meaning. A group of letters added after a word is called a suffix.

Give out **Activity sheet 57 – Suffixes** and ask the children to complete it.

Activity sheet 57 – Suffixes

A number of common suffixes change the meaning of nouns and turn them into adjectives.

   The following suffixes can change nouns into adjectives: *–ish*, *–ful*, *–ly*, *–ous*, *–ic*, *–less*, *–like*, *–y* and *–en*.

Form at least one adjective from this list by adding one of the above suffixes. You may have to alter the spelling slightly, e.g. by changing a final *y* to an *i* or doubling a consonant.

1. cheer _____

2. fool _____

3. life _____

4. glory _____

5. fun _____

6. gold _____

7. hair _____

8. spoon _____

9. day _____

10. fame _____

11. care _____

12. rhythm _____

Turning adjectives into adverbs

Many adjectives are turned into adverbs by adding the suffix –*ly*.

> A suffix consists of letters
> That are added onto a word.
> The suffix –*ly* makes an adverb
> Out of the adjective *absurd*.

Invite groups to do the **Suffix Challenge**. You need to prepare for the game by making a list of common suffixes to give to each player. Your list could be: –*ish*, –*ful*, –*ly*, –*ous*, –*ic*, –*less*, –*like*, –*y* and –*en*.

The Suffix Challenge

This is a game for any number of players. The aim is to think of words which have particular endings. Give each player a list of suffixes and ask everyone to write down one word for each ending. The winner is the first player to write down a word for each ending. An alternative form of the game is to see how many words they can think of which have one particular suffix.

Focus on word formation: compound words

Explain that a compound word is made by joining two words together. For example, note + book forms notebook, and home + work forms homework.

There are hundreds of compound words in the English language. Ask them for examples of other compound word connected with school. Make a list on the board.

Ask the children to play **Compound It**.

Compound It

First they will need to make a set of twenty-eight playing cards with the following words written on them:

> moon day work foot side back horse
> light fall sun man board clothes shoe
> beam ball time way room line shine
> down step high play bed ground door

This is a game for two players. Shuffle the cards, then deal them out equally. Each person then spreads out her cards and makes as many compound words as possible from pairs of cards. They put their leftover cards in the middle of the table and roll a dice. The person with the highest number goes first and tries to make a compound word from the leftover cards. Then it is the other person's turn to try to make a compound word from the leftover words. The game continues until either both players are stuck or all the cards have been used. The winner is the person with the most compound words. If any of the words is disputed, they can look in the dictionary to see if it exists.

Wordplay

This section consists of wordplay games and puzzles. The activities can be given as extension activities to more able pupils, when they have completed a task in a shorter time than the others.

Extension activities

Invite pairs or groups to play **Start and Finish**.

Start and Finish

The aim of the game is to think of words that start and finish with particular letters.

One player asks another player (or the other players) to think of a word that starts with a particular letter and ends with a particular letter. The players then take it in turns to think of such a word. When a round is over, the players can be encouraged to look in a dictionary to find other words that they could have used.

For example, here's what Sasha's friends said when she asked them, 'Can you think of a word that begins with f and ends with l?'

Tim: final
Greg: foul
Kath: fowl
Sasha: fuel
Tim: fail
Greg: fall
Kath: fill
Sasha: full
Tim: fulfil
Greg: fatal

They then were stuck, so after declaring Greg the winner of that round, they looked in the dictionary for any other words beginning with *f* and ending in *l* and found *facial, feudal, foretell, formal* and funnel.

Give out copies of **Activity sheet 58 – I've got a friend** for the pupils to complete. The answers are: alligator antique billboard desperate dandruff elevator jackpot timid tomato valentine. Encourage them to add to the list of friends and to use a dictionary to help them. Show them how they could look up words beginning with *will* and find the word *willpower*. Help them to draft a description, such as: 'I've got a friend. He's strong. He knows his own mind.'

Put the poem 'Animal crackers' on the board. Explain that these are joke definitions. Talk about the play on words in each definition.

Animal crackers

Illegal: a bird of prey that is not very well.
Crowbar: a place where crows meet for a drink
Ramshackle: a sheep that has been tied up.
Bulldozer: a bull which is taking a nap.
Toadstool: an implement used by a toad.

Invite the pupils to create their own **Dictionary of Dotty Definitions**. To get them started, give them copies of **Activity sheet 59 – Dotty definitions**, which is a matching activity.

In this word puzzle, each answer is a word that sounds as if it is a person's name.

The first one has been done for you.

I've got a friend.
She sounds like a person from whom I'm descended. She's called *ancestor.*

I've got a friend.
She's dangerous. She'd snap your head off if you swam near her. She's called _____

I've got a friend.
She's so old that she's a collector's item. She's called _____

I've got a friend.
He's covered in a big advertisement. He's called _____

I've got a friend.
He's given up all hope. He's called _____

I've got a friend.
His hair looks as if it's been sprinkled with white powder. He's called _____

I've got a friend.
She spends all day going up and down. She's called _____

I've got a friend.
He won a huge prize on the lottery. He's called _____

I've got a friend.
He's easily frightened and upset. He's called _____

I've got a friend.
He's red in the face and you'll often find him in a salad. He's called

_____

I've got a friend.
He's an anonymous card that you send to your sweetheart. He's called _____

Try to add some more friends to this list. Think, for example, of words beginning with al, an, bill, del, ele, hal, jack, kit, mark, phil, stan, regi, tom, val and will. Use a dictionary to help you.

Activity sheet 59 – Dotty definitions

Can you match the words to their dotty definitions?

bark	the statue of a cat
barn dance	an old man spouting forth
carrot	a baby ant
caterpillar	a crab
geyser	what you wash your hands in
icicle	the noise made by a wooden dog
infant	the final chapter of a book
nipper	a shed leading a conga
tail end	rust
zinc	a bicycle with a bit missing

Make up some dotty definitions for the words in this list: carpet defiant howl kitbag kipper ponytail recycle.

X is for...

Exclamations

No feature of the English language starts with the letter *x*. But an exclamation sounds as if it does.

An exclamation is a sudden cry or utterance used to express a strong reaction such as surprise, delight or horror.

Focus on exclamations

Explain what an exclamation is and that it is followed by the punctuation mark known as an exclamation mark. An exclamation mark is stronger than a full stop and is used to signal strong feelings or urgency of some kind, e.g. surprise or shock or when telling someone to hurry up or go away.

Put the poem up on the board and talk about how the expressions in it express surprise, delight and horror.

Ask them to draw three columns and to make lists of expressions of surprise, delight and horror that would be followed by an exclamation mark. Include the examples that are given in the poem.

Surprise	**Delight**	**Horror**
Well I never!	Hallelujah!	Oh, no!

Exclamations! Exclamations!

For crying out loud! Well I never!
You could knock me down with a feather!
That's great! Well done!
You're joking! Nice one, son!
Suit yourself! You don't say!
Surely not! No way!
Over my dead body! I told you so!
No kidding! Here we go!

The letter *y* is the 25th letter of the alphabet. It is classified as a consonant, but in a number of words it performs the function of a vowel, e.g. *symbol*, *spy*.

Focus on Y

Make copies of the **Activity sheet 60 – The letter Y** for each pupil or put a copy of the sheet on the whiteboard. Discuss with the class how *y* is used as a vowel and pick out all the examples of this in the poem.

Then ask the pupils to do **Time Challenge (1)**. Words that they could include on their lists are: bygone, bypass, byte, byway, cycle, cylinder, cymbal, dye, dynamo, dynamite, dynasty, gym, gyrate, gypsy, hydrogen, hygiene, hypocrite, lynch, lynx, lyre, myself, mystery, nylon, nymph, psychology, psychiatrist, python, syllable, sympathy, symphony, symptom, type, tyrant, tyre.

Explain that −*y* is sometimes used as a suffix to turn a noun into an adjective. Then ask the pupils to do **Time Challenge (2)**. Words that they could put on their lists include: rainy, windy, cloudy, dusty, stony, sandy, thirsty, tasty, risky, itchy, scratchy, scary, lucky.

Explain that the letter *y* is also sly because it makes two different sounds. It makes the short 'i' sound in words such as *rainy*, *windy* and *itchy*, and the longer 'i' sound in words such as *bygone*, *python* and *tyre*.

Conclude the lesson by explaining that in a few cases, the suffix −*y* turns a verb into a noun. For example, *enquire* becomes *enquiry*. Other examples are: *expire/expiry*, *injure/injury*, *perjure/perjury*.

Y is sly!

Y is sly!

I'll tell you why.

For though y is a consonant,

It can act as a vowel too.

Am I puzzling you?

Think of try, fry and cry,

Spry, wry and dry

And shy and spy and sty.

Think of sympathy, symptom and python,

Of bypass, byway and bygone.

Just to baffle you, it's a suffix too,

Which can turn a noun like sun

Into an adjective sunny

Dirt into dirty and fun into funny.

Are you following me?

It can also be

A suffix which turns

A verb like inquire

Into a noun inquiry,

And it can make injure

Into an injury.

There's more to y than meets the eye.

Y is sly!

Time Challenge (1)

Work in groups. See how many other words in which *y* is used as a vowel you can list in five minutes. Use a dictionary. Note: Fifteen is good. Over twenty is very good. When you have finished, use a dictionary to check any words which are disputed.

The suffix −*y*

At the end of some words −*y* acts as a suffix turning a noun into an adjective.

> Just to baffle you,
> Y is a suffix too,
> Which can turn
> A noun like rain
> Into an adjective rainy,
> Add y to your brain
> And you'll become brainy!

Time Challenge (2)

Make a list of words in which −*y* is used as a suffix to turn a noun into an adjective. Begin your list with the words that are included in the poem. See how many other words you can add to the list in five minutes.

Zed

Z is the last letter of the English alphabet.

Focus on Z

Explain the letter *z* is pronounced 'zed' in Britain but 'zee' in the USA. Ask the children in groups to write down as many words beginning with *z* as they can think of. Collect the words on the board and point out that, if you look in a dictionary, you'll see that there aren't as many English words beginning with the letter *z* as there are words beginning with most other letters.

Put the poem up on the board and talk about the words in it beginning with *z* and what they mean, adding any of them which are not already on it to the list you already have on the board. In addition to the words from the poem, add any of these words that may not already be on the list: *zero, zealot, zig-zag, zodiac, zone, zombie*. Then ask them to write down the words in the order they would appear in a dictionary.

Talk about the sound made by the letter *z*. Put the poem 'Z is a buzz word' on the board and remind them of what onomatopoeia is.

Discuss other words which have double *zz* in them – jazz, pizzazz, razzmatazz, snazzy, dizzy, tizzy, drizzle, fizzle, quizzical, guzzle, muzzle, nuzzle, puzzle, zizz.

Invite them to draft a second verse to add to the poem. For example:

> He's in dizzy and in tizzy,
> He's in snazzy and in jazz,
> He's in drizzle and in fizzle,
> In pizzazz and razzmatazz.

End the session by explaining that in the past, the letter *z* was also called an izzard, but the term has now dropped out of common usage.

Extension activity

Invite more able pupils to write dictionary entries for words beginning with *z* in the order in which they would appear in the dictionary. Tell them to do as many entries as they can without consulting a dictionary, then to use a dictionary to check their definitions and to find out the meaning of those words that they did not know. They can also look up the origin of the words and add them to their entries.

Z's a zipper-zapper

Z's a zipper-zapper.
He's a zebra who's a rapper.

Z can play a zither,
Push a zimmer round the room.
Z's the start of zest and zoo
Of zenith, zinc and zoom.

Z can blow a zephyr
Through the branches of a tree.
In Greek Z stands for zeta.
In the US he's called zee.

Z's the zaniest character you've ever met.
He's number 26 in the alphabet.

Make a list of all the words beginning with z that are included in the poem, putting them in alphabetical order as they would appear in a dictionary and giving their meanings. Use a dictionary to help you with the meanings of any words that you don't know.

Z is a buzz word

The letter *z* helps to make the sound that echoes the meaning in certain onomatopoeic words.

> Z is busy twice in buzzing.
> He's in freezing and in fizz.
> He's in sneezing and in sizzle
> He's in guzzle and in whizz.

Afterword

It is not possible within a book of this length to cover all aspects of the English language, so the focus throughout is on those areas that will give primary age pupils a basic knowledge of English, enabling them to use it confidently and correctly.

It is hoped that the approaches that are suggested will help to enliven the study of language in the primary classroom and will make English lessons enjoyable and interesting for both pupils and teachers.

> After all, when all's said and done,
> The study of English ought to be fun.

Index